CPAG'S

Housing

Council Tax Benefit

Legislation

19th Edition

2006/2007

Supplement

Commentary by
Stewart Wright *MA, Dip. Law, Barrister*

Statutory instruments up to date to 23 May 2007

Published by CPAG, 94 White Lion Street, London N1 9PF

CPAG promotes action for the prevention and relief of poverty among children and families with children. To achieve this, CPAG aims to raise awareness of the causes, extent, nature and impact of poverty, and strategies for its eradication and prevention; bring about positive policy changes for families with children in poverty; and enable those eligible for income maintenance to have access to their full entitlement. If you are not already supporting us, please consider making a donation, or ask for details of our membership schemes and publications.

© CPAG 2007
94 White Lion Street, London N1 9PF

Registered Company No. 1993854
Charity No. 294841

Main work:
ISBN 978 1 901698 91 6
Supplement: ISBN 978 1 901698 92 3

Typeset by David Lewis XML Associates Limited
Printed in Great Britain by William Clowes Limited

Contents

Contents	iii
Introduction	iv
Table of cases	v
Table of commissioners' decisions	v
How to use this supplement	vi
Part I: Noter Up	**1**
Part II: New Regulations	**10**
Housing Benefit and Council Tax Benefit (Amendment) (No. 2) Regulations 2006	10
Housing Benefit and Council Tax Benefit (Electronic Communications) Order 2006	14
Social Security (Miscellaneous Amendments) (No. 5) Regulations 2006	18
Social Security (Bulgaria and Romania) Amendment Regulations 2006	19
Income-related Benefits (Subsidy to Authorities) (Miscellaneous Amendments and Electronic Communications) Order 2007	21
Housing Benefit (Daily Liability Entitlement) Amendment Regulations 2007	32
Rent Repayment Orders (Supplementary Provisions) (England) Regulations 2007	34
Social Security (Miscellaneous Amendments) Regulations 2007	36
Income-related Benefits (Subsidy to Authorities) Amendment Order 2007	39

Introduction

This has been a relatively quiet time for housing benefit and council tax benefit law, both in terms of statutory changes and caselaw. In respect of the former, perhaps the key change has been the Government's change to the advance claims rules (in, for example, regulation 83(10) of the HB Regs 2006), so as to exclude their operation in respect of the habitual residence and right to reside test. Somewhat depressingly, but not unfamiliarly, the cogent and telling criticism of the need for this change made by the Social Security Advisory Committee was ignored by the Government. The result is that if a person is not habitually resident at the date of the HB and CTB decision benefit must, in effect, be refused and a new claim made for the future, notwithstanding that it may be obvious that the person will become habitually resident within the 13 week period after the date of the first claim.

As for the latter, the Tribunal of Commissioners in *CIS 624 2006* has endorsed a common sense but fair approach to decision making by tribunal, holding that although a tribunal should deal with all issues raised by an appeal it need not make a decision on all such issues if there is a better way in which they may be addressed. So, for example, a decision allowing an appeal against a refusal of benefit under regulation 9 of the HB Regs 2006 of itself (and without more) does not mean that the person is then entitled to HB, as there may be other aspects of entitlement (eg, the level of the claimant's capital) which remain to be addressed; and a tribunal is not required to address those issues (eg, the level of capital) if they have not already been addressed by the local authority. However, an authority in its submission to the appeal tribunal should make it plain whether there are any other entitlement issue to be addressed and whether it wants the tribunal to address them (in the absence of such issues, presumably, the tribunal could say that the effect of its allowing the appeal was that the claimant was entitled), and an appeal tribunal in its decision, and an appeal tribunal in its decision should make it clear what the effect of its decision is (ie, whether it is awarding benefit by its decision or has remitted other issues which may affect entitlement to the local authority). It remains to be seen whether either of these two instructions are adopted with any degree of regularity.

Once again my thanks to my colleague Carolyn George for keeping a track of all the legislation found in this supplement, and to James March and Nicola Johnston for their supportive editing. The commentary in the noter-up remains my sole responsibility. Comments or suggestions, either in respect of the supplement or the main work, can be sent to me at CPAG.

Stewart Wright
MA, Dip Law, Barrister, Legal Officer to Child Poverty Action Group and Deputy District Chairman Social Security Appeal Tribunal.

Table of cases

Bland v Chief Supplementary Benefit Officer [1983] 1 WLR 262, CA... **2**
Cooke v Secretary of State for Social Security [2002] 3 All ER 279... **2**
Donnelly v Secretary of State for Work and Pensions [2007] CSOH 01, 10 January 2007... **2**
Jia v Migrationsverket (Case C-1/05), 9 January 2007, unreported (ECJ)... **3**
Mongan v Department for Social Development [2005] NICA 16, 13 April... **1**
Mooney v Secretary of State for Work and Pensions [2004] SLT 1141... **2**
R v Secretary of State for Social Services ex parte Connolly... **2**
R(Balding) v Secretary of State for Work and Pensions [2007] EWHC 759, 3 April 2007, (Admin)... **5**
Regina (Begum) v Social Security Commissioners [2002] EWHC 401... **2**
Secretary of State for Work and Pensions v Bhakta [2006] EWCA Civ 65, (R(IS) 7/06... **4**

Table of social security commissioners' decisions

CH 2193 2005... **1**
CH 2986 2005... **4**
CH 3860 2005... **3, 3**
CH 4108 2005... **5, 5**
CSHB 873 2005... **2**
CH 1821 2006... **5, 5**
CH 1822 2006... **3**
CH 3450 2006... **2**
CH 3629 2006... **4**
CH 3811 2006... **8**
CIS 1757 2006... **3**
CIS 624 2006... **iv, 1**
R 3/05 (DLA)... **1**
R(FC) 1/91... **3**
R(H) 3/07... **2**
R(IB) 2/04... **5**
R(IB) 2/07... **1**

How to use this supplement

Use the Noter-up to find out about changes to the main volume. The page numbers on the left refer to pages in the main volume. The entry opposite either states what the change is or refers to another part of this supplement where the amending legislation is set out.

For abbreviations, see the table on pxxxvi of the main volume.

PART 1: NOTER UP

General

The amounts for, for example, personal allowances, premiums, non-dependant deductions and deductions from rent are confirmed/uprated by the Social Security Benefits Up-rating Order 2007 SI No. 688 as from 1 April 2007 (2 April 2007 for HB payable weekly or in multiples of a week). See Part II for details.

pp35-38   SSAA 1992 s75

[p38: after the first sentence under 'Subsection (3): Recovery from whom?' insert:]

Section 75(3) is wide enough to authorise recovery from a landlord's agent if the overpaid benefit was paid to that agent, notwithstanding that, as an agent, s/he may have accounted to her/his principal (ie, the landlord) for all or part of the sum: *CH 2193 2005*.

pp88-89   SSSAA Part XIII

[p89: delete the final sentence in the second full paragraph on the page (the paragraph beginning 'The significance . . . ') and replace with:]

The correct approach to determining whether the SSAC was misled is to look at all the material placed before the SSAC by the Secretary of State as the basis for the amendment (including answers given by DWP officials to the SSAC) and consider whether the overall effect was misleading; and, if it was, whether there is a real possibility that (a) the information might have misled the SSAC as to the effect of the proposed regulation, and (b) had the SSAC been aware of the regulations true effect it would have wished to have the proposed regulation formally referred to it: *R(IB) 2/07*.

pp145-151   CSPSSA Sch 7 para 6

[p146: delete the whole of the first paragraph under 'The basic approach to decision-making by tribunals' and insert a new penultimate paragraph under that sub-heading (ie, before 'For a more detailed discussion...']

Although (see below) a tribunal should consider every issue that is raised by the appeal, and that will include any issue that is "clearly apparent from the evidence" (per *Mongan v Department for Social Development* [2005] NICA 16, 13 April (reported as *R 3/05 (DLA)*), it does not follow that the tribunal must make a *decision* on *every* issue raised by the appeal if there is a more appropriate way of dealing with one or more issues: *CIS 624 2006*. The Tribunal of Commissioners in that appeal went on to say:

> "When an appeal against an outcome decision raises one issue on which the appeal is allowed but it is necessary to deal with a further issue before another outcome decision is substituted, a tribunal may set aside the original outcome decision without substituting another outcome decision, provided it deals with the original issue raised by the appeal and substitutes a decision on that issue".

It will then be for the Respondent authority to make a fresh decision on the new issue, against which new appeal rights will arise.

The Tribunal of Commissioners gave the following guidance:

- in order to assist tribunals, the [Respondent's] submission to a tribunal should indicate whether it is considered that, if the appeal is allowed, there are any outstanding issues that need further consideration and whether the [Respondent] wishes the tribunal to deal with them;

- where a tribunal, having dealt with the issues originally raised in an appeal, is not able immediately to give an outcome decision, it must decide whether to adjourn or whether to remit the question of entitlement to the [Respondent] if [it] would be in a better position to decide the issue and to seek further information from the claimant;
- the tribunal's decision, as recorded on the decision notice issued at the conclusion of the hearing, should explicitly record what has and has not been decided and in particular, should make it absolutely clear whether the tribunal has made an outcome decision or has remitted the final decision on entitlement to the [Respondent authority].

pp152-159 CSPSSA Sch 7 para 8

[p158: at the end of the analysis under Sub-para (7) add:]

Where leave to appeal is refused by both the appeal tribunal and the commissioner the only remedy for the aggrieved party is judicial review of the commissioner's refusal of leave to appeal: *Bland v Chief Supplementary Benefit Officer* [1983] 1 WLR 262, CA. However, *Donnelly v Secretary of State for Work and Pensions* [2007] CSOH 01, 10 January 2007, makes it plain that, if on an application for judicial review a party raises a point which was not before the commissioner on the application for leave to appeal, the point which is raised must be one which is obvious and has strong prospects of success (following *Regina (Begum) v Social Security Commissioners* [2002] EWHC 401, *Cooke v Secretary of State for Social Security* [2002] 3 All ER 279 and *Mooney v Secretary of State for Work and Pensions* [2004] SLT 1141), and there must have been no other reasons which would have justified the commissioner in refusing leave to appeal: per *R v Secretary of State for Social Services ex parte Connolly* [1986] 1 All ER 998.

pp177-191 HB Regs reg 2

Definitions of "the 2000 Act" and "electronic communication" inserted by Art 2(2) of the Housing Benefit and Council Tax Benefit (Electronic Communications) Order 2006 SI No 2966 as from 20 December 2006.

[p188: delete last sentence of commentary under "long tenancy" (ie, sentence beginning 'Although the . . . ') and replace with:]

An oral agreement cannot create a long tenancy. Moreover, an agreement in writing (but not by deed) will not be enough to create a long tenancy, as sections 52 and 53 of the Law of Property Act 1925 require leases in excess of three years to be made by deed. Accordingly, a written agreement purporting to create a long tenancy but which was not made by deed (ie, under seal), is not a "tenancy granted" for a term in excess of 21 years and is not, therefore, a long tenancy: *R(H) 3/07*.

pp197-207 HB Regs reg 7

Para (6)(d) amended by reg 5 of the Social Security (Miscellaneous Amendments) (No. 5) Regulations 2006 SI No 3274 as from 8 January 2007.

[p204: at the end of the analysis to Sub-para (d)(ie, immediately before Sub-para (e) insert:]

For the position prior to para 6(d)'s amendment from 8 January 2007, see *CSHB 873 2005* where the commissioner construed the pre-amendment form of (what is now) regulation 7(6)(d) as allowing the four weeks of benefit on two homes to be awarded retrospectively back from the date the claimant moved into the second home. The amendment seeks to reverse that result and allow entitlement on two homes only if the liability to pay rent on the two homes exists for four weeks from the date of the move to the second home.

pp213-230 HB Regs reg 9

[p225: at the end of the paragraph 'The motive of the claimant . . . ' add:]

However, although the claimant's perceptions may be relevant as evidence of what is actually possible – so that in an exceptional case a claimant may be under so much stress that it is the interests of her/his own mental health to dispose of ownership as quickly as possible without investigating other possibilities short of sale – it has to be borne in mind that the statutory test to be applied is "could not" and not "believes s/he could not": *CH 3450 2006*.

pp230-31 HB Regs reg 10
Reg 10(3B)(f) substituted by reg 5 of the Social Security (Bulgaria and Romania) Amendment Regulations 2006 SI No 3341 as from 1 January 2007.

pp230-241 HB Regs reg 10

[p239: at the end of paragraph (2) under commentary to Paragraph (3B)(d) add the following:]

A relative of the spouse of an EC national is "dependent" on the latter if s/he is not in a position to support her/himself and has a need for material support in her/his state of origin at the time when applying to join the EC national. A host member state may require proof of this, but a mere undertaking by the EC national or her/his spouse to support the relative will not suffice to establish the existence of real dependence: *Jia v Migrationsverket* (Case C-1/05), 9 January 2007, unreported (ECJ).

pp290-293 HB Regs reg 38

[p292: delete the first sentence (beginning 'For the meaning of . . . ') under Subpara (a)of Paragraph (3)of the Analysis, and replace with:]

In *CH 3860 2005* the commissioner followed *R(FC) 1/91* in holding that the part of the interest on the car loan apportionable to business use could be allowed as an expense "wholly and exclusively incurred . . . for the purposes of [the] employment".

[p292: delete all of the Subpara (c) which is at the bottom of the page.]

[p293: add at the end of the commentary to Subpara (a)under Paragraph 6:]

However, in *CH 3860 2005* the commissioner held that capital repayments in respect of a replacement car are deductible as a car is perfectly capable of amounting to "business equipment or machinery", regardless of how good accounting practice may view it.

pp298-300 HB Regs reg 42
Paragraph (2)(d) substituted by new sub-paragraphs (2)(d) and (da) by reg 6(2) of the Social Security (Miscellaneous Amendments) Regulations 2007 SI No 719 as from 2 April 2007.

pp308-310 HB Regs reg 49
Paragraph (2)(e) substituted by new sub-paragraphs (2)(e) and (ea) by reg 6(3) of the Social Security (Miscellaneous Amendments) Regulations 2007 SI No 719 as from 2 April 2007.

pp308-314 HB Regs reg 49

[p312: delete the first two paragraphs (beginning 'Two HB cases . . . ' and 'Jowitt J . . . ').]

[p313 just above 'Paragraph (2): Capital available on application' insert a new paragraph:]

Note, however, that in some circumstances a claimant may be fixed with notional capital even though the deprivation was by her/his partner *before* they became a couple: *CH 1822 2006* (decided with *CIS 1757 2006*). This is because the focus of regulation 49 is at the time when entitlement is in issue but in respect of a past disposal of capital. In this situation the notional capital rule will only apply to a future partner when there has been conduct that is related to future entitlement to benefit either for the person alone or as a member of a family, and then only when there has been a deprivation of capital with the necessary intention.

p352 HB Regs reg 76
Para (3)(c) substituted and paras (4) and (5) inserted by reg 2(2) of the Housing Benefit (Daily Liability Entitlement) Amendment Regulations 2007 SI No 294 as from 1 April 2007.

pp355-56 HB Regs reg 79
Para (8) amended by reg 2(3) of the Housing Benefit (Daily Liability Entitlement) Amendment Regulations 2007 SI No 294 as from 1 April 2007.

pp364-68 HB Regs reg 83
Paras (1) and (4) amended and paras (4A) to (4E) inserted by reg 2(2) of the Housing Benefit and Council Tax Benefit (Amendment) (No. 2) Regulations 2006 SI No 2967 as from 20 December 2006.

Para (10) substituted by reg 3 of the Social Security, Housing Benefit and Council Tax Benefit (Miscellaneous Amendments) Regulations 2007 SI No 1331 as from 23 May 2007.

[p368: under paragraph 10: Advance claims, for the second sentence substitute the following two sentences:]

If the authority considers that this is likely, and the claimant is not a "person from abroad" (for which see reg 10), providing the known circumstances are fulfilled, it may treat the claimant as claiming in the week before s/he actually becomes entitled: see reg 76(1) for the effect of this. Excluding persons from abroad from this advance claim rule reverses the effect of the Court of Appeal's decision in *Secretary of State for Work and Pensions v Bhakta* [2006] EWCA Civ 65, (*R(IS) 7/06*).

p369 HB Regs new reg 83A
New reg 83A inserted by Art 2(3) of the Housing Benefit and Council Tax Benefit (Electronic Communications) Order 2006 SI No 2966 as from 20 December 2006.

p374 HB Regs reg 87
Amended by reg 2(3) of the Housing Benefit and Council Tax Benefit (Amendment) (No. 2) Regulations 2006 SI No 2967 as from 20 December 2006.

Substituted by reg 6(4) of the Social Security (Miscellaneous Amendments) Regulations 2007 SI No 719 as from 2 April 2007.

p375 HB Regs reg 88
Para (1) amended by reg 2(4) of the Housing Benefit and Council Tax Benefit (Amendment) (No. 2) Regulations 2006 SI No 2967 as from 20 December 2006.

p376 HB Regs new reg 88A
New reg 88A inserted by Art 2(4) of the Housing Benefit and Council Tax Benefit (Electronic Communications) Order 2006 SI No 2966 as from 20 December 2006.

pp386-387 HB Regs reg 94

[p387: Under Analysis, at the beginning insert:]

Once a payment of housing benefit has in fact been made to a claimant under this provision then a second payment may not be made to a landlord covering the same period, even though had the local authority been made aware of the true state of affairs at the time of the payment to the claimant (more than eight weeks' arrears of rent) it would have made the payment instead to the landlord under reg 95(1)(b): *CH 3629 2006* para 39, relying on reg 98 below. However, in most cases this problem should be avoided if local authorities properly notify both parties (ie, landlord and claimant) of the decision changing who is to be paid: see *CH 2986 2005*.

Noter-up

pp387-390   HB Regs reg 95

[p388: after the second sentence under General Note, beginning 'Under this regulation..', add:]

Decisions made under reg 95 may be appealed to an appeal tribunal by either the claimant or the landlord, and it will be an error of law not to invite the claimant or landlord to the hearing of the other parties appeal as both are person's affected by such a decision: *CH 4108 2005*.

[p388: at the end of paragraph (2) under 'Paragraph (1): The duty to pay to the landlord' add:]

Note that what reg 95(1)(b) is concerned with is the tenant being eight weeks or more in arrears of liability for rent; it is not concerned with any set-off from that figure: *CH 4108 2005*. However, the view in that decision that the decision of a local authority as to whether it is in the overriding interest of the claimant not to make direct payments to a landlord may only be interfered with on appeal on judicial review error of law grounds (ie, it is not for the appeal tribunal to decide for itself whether payment direct is not in the overriding interests of the claimant) has, rightly it is suggested, not been followed in *CH 1821 2006*. That later decision makes it plain that on an appeal it is for the appeal tribunal to exercise its normal decision making powers (per *R(IB) 2/04* para 25) on the evidence available and form its own judgment as to whether payment direct is not in the overriding interest of the claimant. *CH 1821 2006* also decides that it is permissible to suspend payment of housing benefit (under regulation 11(2)(a)(ii) of the HB&CTB(D&A) Regs) while enquiries are made as to which person the benefit should be paid to, as a change in payee requires the award to be revised or superseded.

pp407-412   HB Regs reg 102

[p409: at the end of the second paragraph under 'Analysis' add:]

However, if an overpayment decision is made before a person is adjudged bankrupt, it will amount to a "contingent liability" under the Insolvency Act 1986 and a claimant should then be discharged from liability to repay that overpayment under s281 of the Insolvency Act 1986 if and when s/he is discharged from bankruptcy: *R(Balding) v Secretary of State for Work and Pensions* [2007] EWHC 759, 3 April 2007, (Admin) (but note that the decision is under appeal to the Court of Appeal).

[page 411: delete the whole of the paragraph, after (5), beginning 'It is arguable...'.]

pp426-30   HB Regs Sch 1
Paragraph 1(a)(iii) substituted by reg 6(5) of the Social Security (Miscellaneous Amendments) Regulations 2007 SI No 719 as from 2 April 2007.

pp433-47   HB Regs Sch 3
Paragraph 14(6) amended by reg 6(6) of the Social Security (Miscellaneous Amendments) Regulations 2007 SI No 719 as from 2 April 2007.

p497   HB Regs new Sch 11
New Sch 11 inserted by Art 2(5) of the Housing Benefit and Council Tax Benefit (Electronic Communications) Order 2006 SI No 2966 as from 20 December 2006.

pp542-49   CTB Regs reg 2
Definitions of "the 2000 Act" and "electronic communication" inserted by Art 4(2) of the Housing Benefit and Council Tax Benefit (Electronic Communications) Order 2006 SI No 2966 as from 20 December 2006.

Noter-up

pp553-54   CTB Regs reg 7
Reg 7(4A)(f) substituted by reg 7 of the Social Security (Bulgaria and Romania) Amendment Regulations 2006 SI No 3341 as from 1 January 2007.

pp572-75   CTB Regs reg 32
Paragraph (2)(d) substituted by new sub-paragraphs (2)(d) and (da) by reg 8(2) of the Social Security (Miscellaneous Amendments) Regulations 2007 SI No 719 as from 2 April 2007.

pp577-78   CTB Regs reg 39
Paragraph (2)(e) substituted by new sub-paragraphs (2)(e) and (ea) by reg 8(3) of the Social Security (Miscellaneous Amendments) Regulations 2007 SI No 719 as from 2 April 2007.

pp601-04   CTB Regs reg 69
Paras (1) and (4) amended and paras (4A) to (4E) inserted by reg 4(2) of the Housing Benefit and Council Tax Benefit (Amendment) (No. 2) Regulations 2006 SI No 2967 as from 20 December 2006.
Paras (10) and (12) substituted by reg 5 of the Social Security, Housing Benefit and Council Tax Benefit (Miscellaneous Amendments) Regulations 2007 SI No 1331 as from 23 May 2007.

p604   CTB Regs new reg 69A
New reg 69A inserted by Art 4(3) of the Housing Benefit and Council Tax Benefit (Electronic Communications) Order 2006 SI No 2966 as from 20 December 2006.

p607   CTB Regs reg 73
Amended by reg 4(3) of the Housing Benefit and Council Tax Benefit (Amendment) (No. 2) Regulations 2006 SI No 2967 as from 20 December 2006.
Substituted by reg 8(4) of the Social Security (Miscellaneous Amendments) Regulations 2007 SI No 719 as from 2 April 2007.

p607   CTB Regs reg 74
Para (1) amended by reg 4(4) of the Housing Benefit and Council Tax Benefit (Amendment) (No. 2) Regulations 2006 SI No 2967 as from 20 December 2006.

p608   CTB Regs new reg 74A
New reg 74A inserted by Art 4(4) of the Housing Benefit and Council Tax Benefit (Electronic Communications) Order 2006 SI No 2966 as from 20 December 2006.

pp618-25   CTB Regs Sch 1
Paragraph 14(6) amended by reg 8(5) of the Social Security (Miscellaneous Amendments) Regulations 2007 SI No 719 as from 2 April 2007.

p648   CTB Regs new Sch 9
New Sch 9 inserted by Art 4(5) of the Housing Benefit and Council Tax Benefit (Electronic Communications) Order 2006 SI No 2966 as from 20 December 2006.

pp655-63   HB (SPC) Regs reg 2
Definitions of "the 2000 Act" and "electronic communication" inserted by Art 3(2) of the Housing Benefit and Council Tax Benefit (Electronic Communications) Order 2006 SI No 2966 as from 20 December 2006.

pp665-69   HB(SPC) Regs reg 7
Para (6)(d) amended by reg 6 of the Social Security (Miscellaneous Amendments) (No. 5) Regulations 2006 SI No 3274 as from 8 January 2007.

Noter-up

pp671-73   HB(SPC) Regs reg 10
Reg 10(4A)(f) substituted by reg 6 of the Social Security (Bulgaria and Romania) Amendment Regulations 2006 SI No 3341 as from 1 January 2007.

p715   HB (SPC) Regs reg 57
Para (2)(b) substituted and paras (3) and (4) inserted by reg 3(2) of the Housing Benefit (Daily Liability Entitlement) Amendment Regulations 2007 SI No 294 as from 1 April 2007.

pp716-18   HB (SPC) Regs reg 59
Para (8) amended by reg 3(3) of the Housing Benefit (Daily Liability Entitlement) Amendment Regulations 2007 SI No 294 as from 1 April 2007.

pp723-25   HB (SPC) Regs reg 64
Paras (2) and (5) amended and paras (5A) to (5F) inserted by reg 3(2) of the Housing Benefit and Council Tax Benefit (Amendment) (No. 2) Regulations 2006 SI No 2967 as from 20 December 2006.

p726   HB (SPC) Regs new reg 64A
New reg 64A inserted by Art 3(3) of the Housing Benefit and Council Tax Benefit (Electronic Communications) Order 2006 SI No 2966 as from 20 December 2006

p728   HB (SPC) Regs reg 68
Amended by reg 3(3) of the Housing Benefit and Council Tax Benefit (Amendment) (No 2) Regulations 2006 SI No 2967 as from 20 December 2006.
Substituted by reg 7(2) of the Social Security (Miscellaneous Amendments) Regulations 2007 SI No 719 as from 2 April 2007.

pp728-29   HB (SPC) Regs reg 69
Para (1) amended by reg 3(4) of the Housing Benefit and Council Tax Benefit (Amendment) (No. 2) Regulations 2006 SI No 2967 as from 20 December 2006.

p729   HB (SPC) Regs new reg 69A
New reg 69A inserted by Art 3(4) of the Housing Benefit and Council Tax Benefit (Electronic Communications) Order 2006 SI No 2966 as from 20 December 2006.

pp746-48   HB(SPC) Regs Sch 1
Paragraph 1(a)(iii) substituted by reg 7(3) of the Social Security (Miscellaneous Amendments) Regulations 2007 SI No 719 as from 2 April 2007.

pp750-53   HB(SPC) Regs Sch 3
Paragraph 6(8)(a) amended by reg 7(4) of the Social Security (Miscellaneous Amendments) Regulations 2007 SI No 719 as from 2 April 2007.

p777   HB (SPC) Regs new Sch 10
New Sch 10 inserted by Art 3(5) of the Housing Benefit and Council Tax Benefit (Electronic Communications) Order 2006 SI No 2966 as from 20 December 2006.

pp781-87   CTB (SPC) Regs reg 2
Definitions of "the 2000 Act" and "electronic communication" inserted by Art 5(2) of the Housing Benefit and Council Tax Benefit (Electronic Communications) Order 2006 SI No 2966 as from 20 December 2006.

pp789-90   CTB(SPC) Regs reg 7
Reg 7(4A)(f) substituted by reg 8 of the Social Security (Bulgaria and Romania) Amendment Regulations 2006 SI No 3341 as from 1 January 2007.

Noter-up

pp826-28   CTB(SPC) Regs reg 53
Paras (1) and (4) and (5)(e) amended and paras (1ZA) and (4A) to (4F) inserted by reg 5(2) of the Housing Benefit and Council Tax Benefit (Amendment) (No. 2) Regulations 2006 SI No 2967 as from 20 December 2006.
   Paras (10) and (12) substituted by reg 6 of the Social Security, Housing Benefit and Council Tax Benefit (Miscellaneous Amendments) Regulations 2007 SI No 1331 as from 23 May 2007.

pp826-28   CTB (SPC) Regs new reg 53A
New reg 53A inserted by Art 5(3) of the Housing Benefit and Council Tax Benefit (Electronic Communications) Order 2006 SI No 2966 as from 20 December 2006.

p830   CTB (SPC) Regs reg 58
Amended by reg 5(3) of the Housing Benefit and Council Tax Benefit (Amendment) (No. 2) Regulations 2006 SI No 2967 as from 20 December 2006.
   Substituted by reg 9(2) of the Social Security (Miscellaneous Amendments) Regulations 2007 SI No 719 as from 2 April 2007.

pp830-31   CTB (SPC) Regs reg 59
Para (1) amended by reg 5(4) of the Housing Benefit and Council Tax Benefit (Amendment) (No. 2) Regulations 2006 SI No 2967 as from 20 December 2006.

p831   CTB (SPC) Regs new reg 59A
New reg 59A inserted by Art 5(4) of the Housing Benefit and Council Tax Benefit (Electronic Communications) Order 2006 SI No 2966 as from 20 December 2006.

pp840-43   CTB(SPC) Regs Sch 1
Paragraph 6(8)(a) amended by reg 9(3) of the Social Security (Miscellaneous Amendments) Regulations 2007 SI No 719 as from 2 April 2007.

p857   CTB (SPC) Regs new Sch 8
New Sch 8 inserted by Art 5(5) of the Housing Benefit and Council Tax Benefit (Electronic Communications) Order 2006 SI No 2966 as from 20 December 2006.

pp1053-57   HB and CTB (Consequential Provisions) Regulations 2006 Sch 3 para 4

[p1057: at end of commentary under Exempt accommodation add:]

The same commissioner in a later decision, *CH 3811 2006*, emphasises that if the landlord is providing the care, support or supervision s/he need not be the main provider, nor must s/he be providing it pursuant to some contractual or statutory obligation; but the care support or supervision provided by the landlord must be more than a token or minimal amount.

p1088   The Rent Repayment Orders (Supplementary Provisions) (England) Regulations 2007, SI 2007 No 572
Came into force 6 April 2007.

p1094   Income-Related Benefits (Subsidy to Authorities) Order 1998 Art 2
Amended by Art 2(2) of the Income-related Benefits (Subsidy to Authorities) (Miscellaneous Amendments and Electronic Communications) Order 2007 SI No 26 as from 1 February 2007.

p1094   Income-Related Benefits (Subsidy to Authorities) Order 1998 Art 3A
New Art 3A inserted by Art 2(3) of the Income-related Benefits (Subsidy to Authorities) (Miscellaneous Amendments and Electronic Communications) Order 2007 SI No 26 as from 1 February 2007.

pp1094-95   Income-Related Benefits (Subsidy to Authorities) Order 1998 Art 4
Amended by Art 2(4) of the Income-related Benefits (Subsidy to Authorities) (Miscellaneous Amendments and Electronic Communications) Order 2007 SI No 26 as from 1 February 2007 (but in para (2)(c) and (3) only, with retrospective effect from 1 April 2005).

p1095   Income-Related Benefits (Subsidy to Authorities) Order 1998 Art 5
Amended by Art 2(5) of the Income-related Benefits (Subsidy to Authorities) (Miscellaneous Amendments and Electronic Communications) Order 2007 SI No 26 as from 1 February 2007.

p1096   Income-Related Benefits (Subsidy to Authorities) Order 1998 Art 6
Amended by Art 2(6) of the Income-related Benefits (Subsidy to Authorities) (Miscellaneous Amendments and Electronic Communications) Order 2007 SI No 26 as from 1 February 2007.

pp1107-10   Income-Related Benefits (Subsidy to Authorities) Order 1998 Art 18
Amended by Art 3(1) of the Income-related Benefits (Subsidy to Authorities) (Miscellaneous Amendments and Electronic Communications) Order 2007 SI No 26 with retrospective effect from 1 April 2005.

p1114   Income-Related Benefits (Subsidy to Authorities) Order 1998 Art 23
Amended by Art 3(2) of the Income-related Benefits (Subsidy to Authorities) (Miscellaneous Amendments and Electronic Communications) Order 2007 SI No 26 with retrospective effect from 1 April 2005.

pp1115-21   Income-Related Benefits (Subsidy to Authorities) Order 1998 Sch 1
Substituted by Art 4(1) of the Income-related Benefits (Subsidy to Authorities) (Miscellaneous Amendments and Electronic Communications) Order 2007 SI No 26 with retrospective effect from 1 April 2005.

pp1122-29   Income-Related Benefits (Subsidy to Authorities) Order 1998 Sch 4
Amended by Art 4(2) of the Income-related Benefits (Subsidy to Authorities) (Miscellaneous Amendments and Electronic Communications) Order 2007 SI No 26 with retrospective effect from 1 April 2004.

pp1129-34   Income-Related Benefits (Subsidy to Authorities) Order 1998 Sch 4A
Amended by Art 4(3) of the Income-related Benefits (Subsidy to Authorities) (Miscellaneous Amendments and Electronic Communications) Order 2007 SI No 26 with retrospective effect from 1 April 2006.
    Amended by Art 2 and Sch to the Income-related Benefits (Subsidy to Authorities) Amendment Order 2007 SI No 731 as from 1 April 2007.

p1135   Income-Related Benefits (Subsidy to Authorities) Order 1998 Sch 6
Inserted by Art 4(4) of the Income-related Benefits (Subsidy to Authorities) (Miscellaneous Amendments and Electronic Communications) Order 2007 SI No 26 as from 5 February 2007.

PART II: NEW REGULATIONS

The Housing Benefit and Council Tax Benefit (Amendment) (No. 2) Regulations 2006
(SI 2006 No. 2967)

Citation and commencement
1. These Regulations may be cited as the Housing Benefit and Council Tax Benefit (Amendment) (No. 2) Regulations 2006 and shall come into force on 20th December 2006.

Amendment of the Housing Benefit Regulations 2006
2.–(1) The Housing Benefit Regulations 2006 are amended as follows.
(2) In regulation 83 (time and manner in which claims are to be made)–
(a) in paragraph (1) before "Every claim" insert "Subject to paragraph (4A),";
(b) in paragraph (4) after "claim", the first time it appears, insert "in writing"; and
(c) after paragraph (4) insert–

" (4A) Where the relevant authority has published a telephone number for the purpose of receiving claims for housing benefit, a claim may be made by telephone to that telephone number.

(4B) The relevant authority may determine, in any particular case, that a claim made by telephone is not a valid claim unless the person making the claim approves a written statement of his circumstances, provided for the purpose by the relevant authority.

(4C) A claim made by telephone in accordance with paragraph (4A) is defective unless the relevant authority is provided during that telephone call with all the information it requires to determine the claim.

(4D) Where a claim made by telephone in accordance with paragraph (4A) is defective, the relevant authority is to provide the person making it with an opportunity to correct the defect.

(4E) If the person corrects the defect within one month, or such longer period as the relevant authority considers reasonable, of the date it last drew attention to it, the relevant authority shall treat the claim as if it had been duly made in the first instance.".

(3) In regulation 87 (amendment and withdrawal of claim) after "designated office" insert ", except where the claim was made by telephone in accordance with regulation 83(4A) where the amendment may be made by telephone,".

(4) In regulation 88(1) (duty to notify changes of circumstances)–
(a) omit "in writing"; and
(b) after "to the designated office" add–

" (a) in writing or, where the relevant authority has published a telephone number for the purposes of regulation 83 (time and manner in which claims are to be made), by telephone unless the authority determines, in any particular case, that notice must be in writing or may be given otherwise than in writing or by telephone; or
(b) in writing if in any class of case the relevant authority requires written notice unless the authority determines, in any particular case, that notice may be given otherwise than in writing.".

(SI 2006 No.2967, reg 4)

Amendment of the Housing Benefit (Persons who have attained the qualifying age for state pension credit) Regulations 2006

3.–(1) The Housing Benefit (Persons who have attained the qualifying age for state pension credit) Regulations 2006 are amended as follows.

(2) In regulation 64 (time and manner in which claims are to be made)–
  (a) in paragraph (2) before "Every claim" insert "Subject to paragraph (5A) and (5B),";
  (b) in paragraph (5) after "claim", the first time it appears, insert "in writing"; and
  (c) after paragraph (5) insert–

" (5A) Where the relevant authority has published a telephone number for the purpose of receiving claims for housing benefit a claim may be made by telephone to that telephone number.

(5B) A person who is making a claim for state pension credit in accordance with regulation 4D(6A) of the Social Security (Claims and Payments) Regulations 1987[4] may make his claim for housing benefit to the Secretary of State.

(5C) The relevant authority may determine, in any particular case, that a claim made by telephone is not a valid claim unless the person making the claim approves a written statement of his circumstances, provided for the purpose by the relevant authority or the Secretary of State.

(5D) A claim made by telephone in accordance with paragraph (5A) or (5B) is defective unless the relevant authority or the Secretary of State, as the case may be, is provided during that telephone call with all the information the relevant authority requires to determine the claim.

(5E) Where a claim made by telephone in accordance with paragraph (5A) or (5B) is defective, the relevant authority is to provide the person making it with an opportunity to correct the defect.

(5F) If the person corrects the defect within one month, or such longer period as the relevant authority considers reasonable, of the date the relevant authority last drew attention to it, the relevant authority shall treat the claim as if it had been duly made in the first instance.".

(3) In regulation 68 (amendment and withdrawal of claim) after "designated office" insert ", except where the claim was made by telephone in accordance with regulation 64(5A) or (5B) where the amendment may be made by telephone,".

(4) In regulation 69(1) (duty to notify changes of circumstances)–
  (a) omit "in writing"; and
  (b) after "to the designated office" add–

" (a) in writing or, where the relevant authority has published a telephone number for the purposes of regulation 64 (time and manner in which claims are to be made), by telephone unless the authority determines, in any particular case, that notice must be in writing or may be given otherwise than in writing or by telephone; or
  (b) in writing if in any class of case the relevant authority requires written notice unless the authority determines, in any particular case, that notice may be given otherwise than in writing.".

Amendment of the Council Tax Benefit Regulations 2006

4.–(1) The Council Tax Benefit Regulations 2006 are amended as follows.
  (2) In regulation 69 (time and manner in which claims are to be made)–
  (a) in paragraph (1) before "Every claim" insert "Subject to paragraph (4A),";
  (b) in paragraph (4) after "claim", the first time it appears, insert "in writing"; and

(c) after paragraph (4) insert–

"(4A) Where the relevant authority has published a telephone number for the purpose of receiving claims for council tax benefit, a claim may be made by telephone to that telephone number.

(4B) The relevant authority may determine, in any particular case, that a claim made by telephone is not a valid claim unless the person making the claim approves a written statement of his circumstances, provided for the purpose by the relevant authority.

(4C) A claim made by telephone in accordance with paragraph (4A) is defective unless the relevant authority is provided during that telephone call with all the information it requires to determine the claim.

(4D) Where a claim made by telephone in accordance with paragraph (4A) is defective, the relevant authority is to provide the person making it with an opportunity to correct the defect.

(4E) If the person corrects the defect within one month, or such longer period as the relevant authority considers reasonable, of the date it last drew attention to it, the relevant authority shall treat the claim as if it had been duly made in the first instance.".

(3) In regulation 73 (amendment and withdrawal of claim) after "designated office" insert ", except where the claim was made by telephone in accordance with regulation 69(4A) where the amendment may be made by telephone,".

(4) In regulation 74(1) (duty to notify changes of circumstances)–
(a) omit "in writing"; and
(b) after "to the designated office" add–

" (a) in writing or, where the relevant authority has published a telephone number for the purposes of regulation 69 (time and manner in which claims are to be made), by telephone unless the authority determines, in any particular case, that notice must be in writing or may be given otherwise than in writing or by telephone; or
(b) in writing if in any class of case the relevant authority requires written notice unless the authority determines, in any particular case, that notice may be given otherwise than in writing.".

Amendment of the Council Tax Benefit (Persons who have attained the qualifying age for state pension credit) Regulations 2006

5.–(1) The Council Tax Benefit (Persons who have attained the qualifying age for state pension credit) Regulations 2006 are amended as follows.

(2) In regulation 53 (time and manner in which claims are to be made)–
(a) at the beginning insert–

"(1ZA) The prescribed time for claiming council tax benefit is as regards any day on which, apart from satisfying the condition of making a claim, the claimant is entitled to council tax benefit, that day and the period of twelve months immediately following it.";

(b) in paragraph (1) before "Every claim" insert "Subject to paragraph (4A) and (4B),";
(c) in paragraph (4) after "claim", the first time it appears, insert "in writing";
(d) after paragraph (4) insert–

"(4A) Where the relevant authority has published a telephone number for the purpose of receiving claims for council tax benefit, a claim may be made by telephone to that telephone number.

(4B) A person who is making a claim for state pension credit in accordance with regulation 4D(6A) of the Social Security (Claims and Payments) Regulations 1987 may make his claim for council tax benefit to the Secretary of State.

(4C) The relevant authority may determine, in any particular case, that a claim made by telephone is not a valid claim unless the person making the claim approves a written statement of his circumstances, provided for the purpose by the relevant authority or the Secretary of State.

(4D) A claim made by telephone in accordance with paragraph (4A) or (4B) is defective unless the relevant authority or the Secretary of State, as the case may be, is provided during that telephone call with all the information the relevant authority requires to determine the claim.

(4E) Where a claim made by telephone in accordance with paragraph (4A) or (4B) is defective, the relevant authority is to provide the person making it with an opportunity to correct the defect.

(4F) If the person corrects the defect within one month, or such longer period as the relevant authority considers reasonable, of the date it last drew attention to it, the relevant authority shall treat the claim as if it had been duly made in the first instance.''; and

    (e)   in sub-paragraph (5)(e) after ''designated office'' add ''or authorised office or appropriate DWP office''.

(3) In regulation 58 (amendment and withdrawal of claim) after ''designated office'' insert '', except where the claim was made by telephone in accordance with regulation 53(4A) or (4B) where the amendment may be made by telephone,''.

(4) In regulation 59(1) (duty to notify changes of circumstances)–
    (a)   omit ''in writing''; and
    (b)   after ''to the designated office'' add–

'' (a) in writing or, where the relevant authority has published a telephone number for the purposes of regulation 53 (time and manner in which claims are to be made), by telephone unless the authority determines, in any particular case, that notice must be in writing or may be given otherwise than in writing or by telephone; or

    (b)   in writing if in any class of case the relevant authority requires written notice unless the authority determines, in any particular case, that notice may be given otherwise than in writing.''.

The Housing Benefit and Council Tax Benefit (Electronic Communications) Order 2006
(SI 2006 No. 2968)

Citation and commencement
1. This Order may be cited as the Housing Benefit and Council Tax Benefit (Electronic Communications) Order 2006 and shall come into force on 20th December 2006.

Amendment of the Housing Benefit Regulations 2006
2.–(1) The Housing Benefit Regulations 2006 are amended as follows.
(2) In regulation 2(1) (interpretation)–
(a) after the definition of "the 1973 Act" insert–

" "the 2000 Act" means the Electronic Communications Act 2000;"; and

(b) after the definition of "the Eileen Trust" insert–

" "electronic communication" has the same meaning as in section 15(1) of the 2000 Act;".

(3) After regulation 83 (time and manner in which claims are to be made) insert–

" **Electronic claims for benefit**
83A. A claim for housing benefit may be made by means of an electronic communication in accordance with Schedule 11.".

(4) After regulation 88 (duty to notify changes of circumstances) insert–

" **Notice of changes of circumstances given electronically**
88A. A person may give notice of a change of circumstances required to be notified under regulation 88 by means of an electronic communication in accordance with Schedule 11.".

(5) After Schedule 10 (prescribed authorities) insert as Schedule 11 the Schedule set out in the Schedule to this Order.

Amendment of the Housing Benefit (Persons who have attained the qualifying age for state pension credit) Regulations 2006
3.–(1) The Housing Benefit (Persons who have attained the qualifying age for state pension credit) Regulations 2006 are amended as follows.
(2) In regulation 2(1) (interpretation)–
(a) after the definition of "the 1973 Act" insert–

" "the 2000 Act" means the Electronic Communications Act 2000;"; and

(b) after the definition of "the Eileen Trust" insert–

" "electronic communication" has the same meaning as in section 15(1) of the 2000 Act;".

(3) After regulation 64 (time and manner in which claims are to be made) insert–

" **Electronic claims for benefit**
64A. A claim for housing benefit may be made by means of an electronic communication in accordance with Schedule 10.".

(SI 2006 No.2968, reg 5)

(4) After regulation 69 (duty to notify changes of circumstances) insert–

" **Notice of changes of circumstances given electronically**
69A. A person may give notice of a change of circumstances required to be notified under regulation 69 by means of an electronic communication in accordance with Schedule 10.".

(5) After Schedule 9 (prescribed authorities) insert as Schedule 10 the Schedule set out in the Schedule to this Order.

Amendment of the Council Tax Benefit Regulations 2006

4.–(1) The Council Tax Benefit Regulations 2006 are amended as follows.
(2) In regulation 2(1) (interpretation)–
(a) after the definition of "the 1992 Act" insert–

" "the 2000 Act" means the Electronic Communications Act 2000;"; and

(b) after the definition of "the Eileen Trust" insert–

" "electronic communication" has the same meaning as in section 15(1) of the 2000 Act;".

(3) After regulation 69 (time and manner in which claims are to be made) insert–

" **Electronic claims for benefit**
69A. A claim for council tax benefit may be made by means of an electronic communication in accordance with Schedule 9.".

(4) After regulation 74 (duty to notify changes of circumstances) insert–

" **Notice of changes of circumstances given electronically**
74A. A person may give notice of a change of circumstances required to be notified under regulation 74 by means of an electronic communication in accordance with Schedule 9.".

(5) After Schedule 8 (prescribed authorities) insert as Schedule 9 the Schedule set out in the Schedule to this Order.

Amendment of the Council Tax Benefit (Persons who have attained the qualifying age for state pension credit) Regulations 2006

5.–(1) The Council Tax Benefit (Persons who have attained the qualifying age for state pension credit) Regulations 2006 are amended as follows.
(2) In regulation 2(1) (interpretation)–
(a) after the definition of "the 1992 Act" insert–

" "the 2000 Act" means the Electronic Communications Act 2000;"; and

(b) after the definition of "the Eileen Trust" insert–

" "electronic communication" has the same meaning as in section 15(1) of the 2000 Act;".

(3) After regulation 53 (time and manner in which claims are to be made) insert–

" **Electronic claims for benefit**
53A. A claim for council tax benefit may be made by means of an electronic communication in accordance with Schedule 8.".

(4) After regulation 59 (duty to notify changes of circumstances) insert–

" **Notice of changes of circumstances given electronically**
59A. A person may give notice of a change of circumstances required to be notified under regulation 59 by means of an electronic communication in accordance with Schedule 8.".

(5) After Schedule 7 (prescribed authorities) insert as Schedule 8 the Schedule set out in the Schedule to this Order.

SCHEDULE
Articles 2(5), 3(5), 4(5) and 5(5)

" SCHEDULE
ELECTRONIC COMMUNICATION
PART 1
Introduction

Interpretation
1. In this Schedule "official computer system" means a computer system maintained by or on behalf of the relevant authority or of the Secretary of State for sending, receiving, processing or storing of any claim, certificate, notice, information or evidence.

PART 2
Electronic Communication – General Provisions

Conditions for the use of electronic communication
2.–(1) The relevant authority may use an electronic communication in connection with claims for, and awards of, benefit under these Regulations.
(2) A person other than the relevant authority may use an electronic communication in connection with the matters referred to in sub-paragraph (1) if the conditions specified in sub-paragraphs (3) to (6) are satisfied.
(3) The first condition is that the person is for the time being permitted to use an electronic communication by an authorisation given by means of a direction of the Chief Executive of the relevant authority.
(4) The second condition is that the person uses an approved method of–
(a) authenticating the identity of the sender of the communication;
(b) electronic communication;
(c) authenticating any claim or notice delivered by means of an electronic communication; and
(d) subject to sub-paragraph (7), submitting to the relevant authority any claim, certificate, notice, information or evidence.
(5) The third condition is that any claim, certificate, notice, information or evidence sent by means of an electronic communication is in a form approved for the purposes of this Schedule.
(6) The fourth condition is that the person maintains such records in written or electronic form as may be specified in a direction given by the Chief Executive of the relevant authority.
(7) Where the person uses any method other than the method approved of submitting any claim, certificate, notice, information or evidence, that claim, certificate, notice, information or evidence shall be treated as not having been submitted.
(8) In this paragraph "approved" means approved by means of a direction given by the Chief Executive of the relevant authority for the purposes of this Schedule.

Use of intermediaries
3. The relevant authority may use intermediaries in connection with–
(a) the delivery of any claim, certificate, notice, information or evidence by means of an electronic communication; and
(b) the authentication or security of anything transmitted by such means,
and may require other persons to use intermediaries in connection with those matters.

(SI 2006 No.2968, reg 5)

PART 3
Electronic Communication – Evidential Provisions

Effect of delivering information by means of electronic communication

4.–(1) Any claim, certificate, notice, information or evidence which is delivered by means of an electronic communication shall be treated as having been delivered in the manner or form required by any provision of these Regulations, on the day the conditions imposed–
(a)   by this Schedule; and
(b)   by or under an enactment,
are satisfied.
(2) The relevant authority may, by a direction, determine that any claim, certificate, notice, information or evidence is to be treated as delivered on a different day (whether earlier or later) from the day provided for in sub-paragraph (1).
(3) Information shall not be taken to have been delivered to an official computer system by means of an electronic communication unless it is accepted by the system to which it is delivered.

Proof of identity of sender or recipient of information

5. If it is necessary to prove, for the purpose of any legal proceedings, the identity of–
(a)   the sender of any claim, certificate, notice, information or evidence delivered by means of an electronic communication to an official computer system; or
(b)   the recipient of any such claim, certificate, notice, information or evidence delivered by means of an electronic communication from an official computer system,
the sender or recipient, as the case may be, shall be presumed to be the person whose name is recorded as such on that official computer system.

Proof of delivery of information

6.–(1) If it is necessary to prove, for the purpose of any legal proceedings, that the use of an electronic communication has resulted in the delivery of any claim, certificate, notice, information or evidence this shall be presumed to have been the case where–
(a)   any such claim, certificate, notice, information or evidence has been delivered to the relevant authority, if the delivery of that claim, certificate, notice, information or evidence has been recorded on an official computer system; or
(b)   any such claim, certificate, notice, information or evidence has been delivered by the relevant authority, if the delivery of that certificate, notice, information or evidence has been recorded on an official computer system.
(2) If it is necessary to prove, for the purpose of any legal proceedings, that the use of an electronic communication has resulted in the delivery of any such claim, certificate, notice, information or evidence, this shall be presumed not to be the case, if that claim, certificate, notice, information or evidence delivered to the relevant authority has not been recorded on an official computer system.
(3) If it is necessary to prove, for the purpose of any legal proceedings, when any such claim, certificate, notice, information or evidence sent by means of an electronic communication has been received, the time and date of receipt shall be presumed to be that recorded on an official computer system.

Proof of content of information

7. If it is necessary to prove, for the purpose of any legal proceedings, the content of any claim, certificate, notice, information or evidence sent by means of an electronic communication, the content shall be presumed to be that recorded on an official computer system.''

The Social Security (Miscellaneous Amendments) (No. 5) Regulations 2006
(SI 2006 No. 3274)

Citation and commencement
1. These Regulations may be cited as the Social Security (Miscellaneous Amendments) (No. 5) Regulations 2006 and shall come into force on 8th January 2007.

Amendment of the Housing Benefit Regulations 2006
5. In regulation 7(6)(d) of the Housing Benefit Regulations 2006 (circumstances in which a person is or is not to be treated as occupying a dwelling as his home), after "4 benefit weeks" insert "from the date on which he moved".

Amendment of the Housing Benefit (Persons who have attained the qualifying age for state pension credit) Regulations 2006
6. In regulation 7(6)(d) of the Housing Benefit (Persons who have attained the qualifying age for state pension credit) Regulations 2006 (circumstances in which a person is or is not to be treated as occupying a dwelling as his home), after "four benefit weeks" insert "from the date on which he moved".

The Social Security (Bulgaria and Romania) Amendment Regulations 2006
(SI 2006 No. 3341)

Citation and commencement
1. These Regulations may be cited as the Social Security (Bulgaria and Romania) Amendment Regulations 2006 and shall come into force on 1st January 2007 (immediately after the Accession (Immigration and Worker Authorisation) Regulations 2006 come into force).

Amendment of the Housing Benefit Regulations 2006
5.–(1) The Housing Benefit Regulations 2006 are amended as follows.
(2) In regulation 10(3B) (persons from abroad), for sub-paragraph (f) substitute–

" (f) a person who is treated as a worker for the purpose of the definition of "qualified person" in regulation 6(1) of the Immigration (European Economic Area) Regulations 2006 pursuant to–
  (i) regulation 5 of the Accession (Immigration and Worker Registration) Regulations 2004 (application of the 2006 Regulations in relation to a national of the Czech Republic, Estonia, Latvia, Lithuania, Hungary, Poland, Slovenia or the Slovak Republic who is an "accession State worker requiring registration"), or
  (ii) regulation 6 of the Accession (Immigration and Worker Authorisation) Regulations 2006 (right of residence of a Bulgarian or Romanian who is an "accession State national subject to worker authorisation");".

Amendment of the Housing Benefit (Persons who have attained the qualifying age for state pension credit) Regulations 2006
6.–(1) The Housing Benefit (Persons who have attained the qualifying age for state pension credit) Regulations 2006 are amended as follows.
(2) In regulation 10(4A) (persons from abroad), for sub-paragraph (f) substitute–

" (f) a person who is treated as a worker for the purpose of the definition of "qualified person" in regulation 6(1) of the Immigration (European Economic Area) Regulations 2006 pursuant to–
  (i) regulation 5 of the Accession (Immigration and Worker Registration) Regulations 2004 (application of the 2006 Regulations in relation to a national of the Czech Republic, Estonia, Latvia, Lithuania, Hungary, Poland, Slovenia or the Slovak Republic who is an "accession State worker requiring registration"), or
  (ii) regulation 6 of the Accession (Immigration and Worker Authorisation) Regulations 2006 (right of residence of a Bulgarian or Romanian who is an "accession State national subject to worker authorisation");".

Amendment of the Council Tax Benefit Regulations 2006
7.–(1) The Council Tax Benefit Regulations 2006 are amended as follows.
(2) In regulation 7(4A) (persons from abroad), for sub-paragraph (f) substitute–

" (f) a person who is treated as a worker for the purpose of the definition of "qualified person" in regulation 6(1) of the Immigration (European Economic Area) Regulations 2006 pursuant to–
  (i) regulation 5 of the Accession (Immigration and Worker Registration) Regulations 2004 (application of the 2006 Regulations in relation to a national of the Czech Republic, Estonia, Latvia, Lithuania, Hungary, Poland, Slovenia or the Slovak Republic who is an "accession State worker requiring registration"), or

(ii) regulation 6 of the Accession (Immigration and Worker Authorisation) Regulations 2006 (right of residence of a Bulgarian or Romanian who is an "accession State national subject to worker authorisation");".

Amendment of the Council Tax Benefit (Persons who have attained the qualifying age for state pension credit) Regulations 2006

8.–(1) The Council Tax Benefit (Persons who have attained the qualifying age for state pension credit) Regulations 2006 are amended as follows.

(2) In regulation 7(4A) (persons from abroad), for sub-paragraph (f) substitute–

" (f) a person who is treated as a worker for the purpose of the definition of "qualified person" in regulation 6(1) of the Immigration (European Economic Area) Regulations 2006 pursuant to–
  (i) regulation 5 of the Accession (Immigration and Worker Registration) Regulations 2004 (application of the 2006 Regulations in relation to a national of the Czech Republic, Estonia, Latvia, Lithuania, Hungary, Poland, Slovenia or the Slovak Republic who is an "accession State worker requiring registration"), or
  (ii) regulation 6 of the Accession (Immigration and Worker Authorisation) Regulations 2006 (right of residence of a Bulgarian or Romanian who is an "accession State national subject to worker authorisation");".

The Income-related Benefits (Subsidy to Authorities) (Miscellaneous Amendments and Electronic Communications) Order 2007
(SI 2007 No. 26)

Citation, commencement, effect and interpretation

1.–(1) This Order may be cited as the Income-related Benefits (Subsidy to Authorities) (Miscellaneous Amendments and Electronic Communications) Order 2007 and shall come into force on 5th February 2007.

(2) Article 4(2) shall have effect from 1st April 2004.

(3) Articles 2(4)(b), 3 and 4(1) shall have effect from 1st April 2005.

(4) Article 4(3) shall have effect from 1st April 2006.

(5) In this Order, "the principal Order" means the Income-related Benefits (Subsidy to Authorities) Order 1998.

Amendment of Part II of the principal Order

2.–(1) Part II of the principal Order (claims for and payment of subsidy) shall be amended in accordance with the following paragraphs.

(2) In article 2 (interpretation of Parts II and IV) after the definition of "claim form", insert–

" "electronic communication" has the same meaning as in section 15(1) of the Electronic Communications Act 2000";

(3) After article 3 (conditions for payment of subsidy), insert–

" **Electronic communications**

3A.–(1) The Secretary of State, an authority or auditor may use an electronic communication in connection with any claim, audit or payment of subsidy provided it is made in accordance with the provisions set out in Part 2 of Schedule 6.

(2) Any reference to an electronic communication in this Order means an electronic communication made in accordance with those provisions.

(3) Schedule 6 makes further provisions relating to electronic communications.".

(4) In article 4 (requirement of claim)–
- (a) in paragraphs (2) and (4) after the words "on the form supplied by him to that authority", insert "or by means of an electronic communication";
- (b) in paragraphs (2)(c) and (3) for "30th June" substitute "31st May";
- (c) in paragraph (3) before the words "The final claim", insert "Except where an authority submits a claim by means of an electronic communication,";
- (d) omit paragraph (4A);
- (e) in paragraph (4B) after the words "on such form as is supplied by him or them", insert "or by means of an electronic communication"; and
- (f) in paragraph (5) after the words "shall be signed", insert "or submitted by means of an electronic communication".

(5) In article 5 (requirement to keep records and provide information)–
- (a) in sub-paragraph (1)(a) after "paragraph (2)", insert "in written or electronic form";
- (b) in sub-paragraph (1)(b) after the words "produce records", insert "in written or electronic form"; and
- (c) in sub-paragraph (2)(a) for "full, accurate and properly calculated", substitute "fairly stated and in accordance with the relevant articles of this Order".

(6) In article 6 (requirement of audit)–

(a) in paragraph (1)(ia) after the words "is submitted to the Secretary of State", insert "in written or electronic form";
(b) in paragraph (2)(a) after the words "such information", insert "in written or electronic form";
(c) for sub-paragraph (b) of paragraph (2) and the words following that paragraph substitute–

"(b) keep, and where asked to do so, produce records in written or electronic form with a bearing on its claim,

as may be required by the auditor or as may be otherwise required to enable that authority to show and its auditor to check, that that claim is fairly stated and in accordance with the relevant articles of this Order."; and

(d) for paragraph (3) substitute–

" (3) No final subsidy shall be paid until the authority's auditor has certified on the claim for or by means of an electronic communication that the final claim is fairly stated and in accordance with the relevant articles of this Order.".

Amendment of Part III of the principal Order

3.–(1) Omit article 18(5)(a) of the principal Order (additions to subsidy).

(2) Omit article 23(2) of the principal Order (transitional provisions in relation to rent officer determinations).

Amendment of the Schedules to the principal Order

4.–(1) For Schedule 1 to the principal Order (sums to be used in the calculation of subsidy) substitute as Schedule 1 the Schedule set out in Schedule 1 to this Order.

(2) In Schedule 4 to the principal Order (high rents and rent allowances)–
(a) in paragraphs 7, 8(3), 9(2) to (5) and 11 of Part 2 (rent officers' determinations); and
(b) in paragraph 15 of Part 3 (reckonable rent cases),

for "95 per cent", substitute "100 per cent".

(3) In Schedule 4A to the principal Order (rent rebate limitation deductions (housing revenue account dwellings))–
(a) in paragraph 2(4) (liability to deduction)–
   (i) in step 1 and 2 for "service charges were imposed" substitute "rent was charged"; and
   (ii) in step 4 for "new service charges were imposed" substitute "rent was charged"
(b) after paragraph 2(7), insert–

" (8) For the purposes of calculating the total number of weeks for which rent is charged in sub-paragraphs (3) and (4) rent free periods shall be included.";

(c) in the table in Part 3 (weekly rent limits for purposes of Part 2: authorities in England), in the entry relating to Dover for "£61.53", substitute "£63.05".

(4) After Schedule 4A to the principal Order insert as Schedule 6 the Schedule set out in Schedule 2 to this Order.

(SI 2007 No.26, Sch 1)

SCHEDULE 1
Article 3
SCHEDULE TO BE SUBSTITUTED FOR SCHEDULE 1 TO THE PRINCIPAL ORDER

" SCHEDULE 1
Articles 12(1)(b) and 17(1) and (8)

SUMS TO BE USED IN THE CALCULATION OF SUBSIDY

	Administration subsidy Threshold (£)	Non-HRA Rent Rebates Cap (£)	(£)
England			
Adur	541,150	117.63	203.30
Allerdale	820,662	94.42	162.87
Alnwick	187,588	81.85	141.83
Amber Valley	2,177,537	94.89	163.87
Arun	801,040	123.12	212.38
Ashfield	694,574	89.10	153.87
Ashford	544,777	116.91	201.88
Aylesbury Vale	553,713	113.05	195.67
Babergh	391,953	108.20	186.83
Barking and Dagenham	3,467,516	223.51	346.99
Barnet	2,459,834	223.51	346.99
Barnsley	1,679,991	79.15	137.65
Barrow in Furness	576,998	98.76	170.54
Basildon	1,197,999	114.95	198.50
Basingstoke and Deane	719,350	117.07	201.95
Bassetlaw	630,003	99.33	171.53
Bath & North East Somerset	1,112,332	100.71	173.73
Bedford	962,281	93.24	161.42
Berwick upon Tweed	184,582	88.60	152.98
Bexley	1,362,860	223.51	346.99
Birmingham	10,721,429	95.47	165.32
Blaby	295,933	85.08	147.23
Blackburn with Darwen	1,550,729	108.94	187.92
Blackpool	2,142,732	90.73	160.83
Blyth Valley	604,122	75.02	129.88
Bolsover	639,470	77.36	136.39
Bolton	2,657,289	81.72	142.4
Boston	411,275	85.21	147.31
Bournemouth	1,474,200	102.41	187.95
Bracknell Forest	493,431	127.2	223.22
Bradford	4,201,293	86.20	158.19
Braintree	670,747	104.64	180.69
Breckland	960,122	107.01	185.25
Brent	3,652,904	223.51	366.97
Brentwood	388,832	118.62	204.84
Bridgnorth	304,791	96.45	167.79
Brighton and Hove	2,451,490	105.84	203.09
Bristol	3,016,186	93.23	180.00
Broadland	564,628	107.01	185.25
Bromley	1,833,635	223.51	346.99
Bromsgrove	599,819	99.45	179.46
Broxbourne	416,427	126.48	218.41
Broxtowe	1,083,155	81.36	141.69
Burnley	963,316	96.75	166.89
Bury	1,259,114	94.23	162.72
Calderdale	1,471,710	83.75	144.71
Cambridge	614,340	111.41	192.38
Camden	3,367,912	223.51	365.30
Cannock Chase	518,977	99.89	178.38
Canterbury	879,676	112.34	193.97
Caradon	455,141	94.69	163.51
Carlisle	908,624	92.14	159.10

Income-related Benefits (Subsidy to Authorities) (Misc Amends and Electronic Comms) Order 2007

	Administration subsidy Threshold (£)	Non-HRA Rent Rebates Cap (£)	(£)
Carrick	546,892	107.83	186.20
Castle Morpeth	202,845	88.89	153.50
Castle Point	673,294	122.30	211.18
Charnwood	584,764	85.61	147.85
Chelmsford	796,312	119.70	207.46
Cheltenham	601,259	121.58	209.93
Cherwell	633,201	117.87	203.82
Chester	847,625	89.00	153.52
Chester le Street	499,581	82.28	142.53
Chesterfield	794,632	81.69	141.06
Chichester	642,039	118.48	204.37
Chiltern	376,484	117.07	201.95
Chorley	481,619	83.82	145.54
Christchurch	264,923	100.71	184.64
City of London	102,295	223.51	346.99
Colchester	804,419	110.25	191.93
Congleton	387,214	94.42	162.87
Copeland	958,391	88.71	164.58
Corby	329,919	91.42	163.13
Cotswold	558,760	100.71	173.73
Coventry	2,977,295	81.21	155.64
Craven	250,835	100.12	172.89
Crawley	563,744	126.74	219.64
Crewe and Nantwich	715,779	99.90	179.69
Croydon	3,439,965	223.51	360.44
Dacorum	741,450	110.97	194.04
Darlington	787,433	86.96	150.16
Dartford	700,602	114.85	198.32
Daventry	242,633	91.32	157.69
Derby	1,907,939	90.19	155.76
Derbyshire Dales	309,095	91.57	158.47
Derwentside	1,047,550	89.71	154.91
Doncaster	2,029,010	82.28	144.48
Dover	870,579	116.94	201.93
Dudley	2,201,242	95.78	167.82
Durham	713,680	84.71	148.23
Ealing	2,370,849	223.51	351.19
Easington	952,559	87.21	150.59
East Cambridgeshire	363,667	107.01	185.25
East Devon	549,226	91.41	167.75
East Dorset	391,512	100.71	184.64
East Hampshire	500,372	117.07	201.95
East Hertfordshire	508,022	127.90	221.65
East Lindsey	957,002	87.82	151.81
East Northamptonshire	412,822	98.10	169.60
East Riding of Yorkshire	1,651,981	87.66	155.41
East Staffordshire	746,426	85.52	147.52
Eastbourne	929,671	105.32	193.31
Eastleigh	497,202	117.07	201.95
Eden	216,951	94.42	162.87
Ellesmere Port and Neston	681,717	73.57	145.96
Elmbridge	683,799	133.53	230.32
Enfield	2,962,511	223.51	346.99
Epping Forest	574,529	113.34	196.26
Epsom and Ewell	239,878	117.07	201.95
Erewash	606,111	83.97	145.31
Exeter	793,266	88.54	162.50
Fareham	315,483	110.95	195.45
Fenland	548,408	100.56	173.66
Forest Heath	213,305	99.04	171.03
Forest of Dean	705,851	96.52	166.67

(SI 2007 No.26, Sch 1)

	Administration subsidy Threshold (£)	Non-HRA Rent Rebates Cap (£)	(£)
Fylde	373,689	82.51	142.31
Gateshead	4,151,653	87.29	150.74
Gedling	550,834	83.14	144.18
Gloucester	720,049	105.41	182.02
Gosport	418,312	108.81	187.90
Gravesham	916,856	111.04	191.76
Great Yarmouth	1,267,467	83.55	153.34
Greenwich	3,455,031	223.51	346.99
Guildford	508,357	134.07	231.52
Hackney	4,098,097	223.51	347.48
Halton	1,405,420	86.83	155.33
Hambleton	535,304	83.08	152.54
Hammersmith and Fulham	2,405,655	223.51	346.99
Harborough	428,222	103.09	178.01
Haringey	2,767,088	223.51	346.99
Harlow	579,851	109.42	188.94
Harrogate	585,388	106.57	184.04
Harrow	1,307,876	223.51	381.29
Hart	513,841	117.07	201.95
Hartlepool	1,182,656	90.16	155.69
Hastings	1,018,078	117.07	201.95
Havant	642,013	117.07	201.95
Havering	1,249,238	223.51	346.99
Herefordshire	1,117,571	89.64	154.80
Hertsmere	530,671	107.01	185.25
High Peak	449,673	96.94	167.39
Hillingdon	1,591,178	223.51	383.39
Hinckley and Bosworth	356,258	93.60	161.64
Horsham	703,607	138.41	238.74
Hounslow	1,569,795	223.51	346.99
Huntingdonshire	725,955	115.92	200.68
Hyndburn	656,521	93.45	161.20
Ipswich	929,602	99.72	172.19
Isle of Wight	1,076,317	117.07	201.95
Isles of Scilly	7,951	104.08	179.73
Islington	3,485,205	223.51	359.52
Kennet	359,786	100.71	173.73
Kensington and Chelsea	2,158,521	223.51	396.15
Kerrier	810,317	100.71	173.73
Kettering	404,257	90.21	157.06
Kings Lynn and West Norfolk	1,024,778	87.62	159.42
Kingston upon Hull	3,087,282	90.63	162.38
Kingston upon Thames	695,047	223.51	372.60
Kirklees	2,566,641	91.86	158.64
Knowsley	2,069,706	102.02	176.17
Lambeth	4,509,682	223.51	346.99
Lancaster	902,217	90.85	156.87
Leeds	6,087,011	83.41	153.46
Leicester	3,156,743	92.52	159.61
Lewes	492,190	113.59	197.50
Lewisham	4,044,602	223.51	346.99
Lichfield	606,649	92.82	160.12
Lincoln	796,442	87.56	151.20
Liverpool	6,165,922	93.12	160.83
Luton	1,292,893	114.55	197.81
Macclesfield	645,726	103.10	193.20
Maidstone	762,416	116.30	200.82
Maldon	306,138	107.01	185.25
Malvern Hills	464,980	92.82	160.12
Manchester	5,994,281	109.17	188.51
Mansfield	739,362	93.71	161.65

Income-related Benefits (Subsidy to Authorities) (Misc Amends and Electronic Comms) Order 2007

	Administration subsidy Threshold (£)	Non-HRA Rent Rebates Cap (£)	(£)
Medway	1,576,395	114.85	198.32
Melton	159,782	84.14	149.23
Mendip	769,027	99.23	171.18
Merton	1,048,254	223.51	346.99
Mid Bedfordshire	665,055	106.32	184.26
Mid Devon	367,375	94.27	162.80
Mid Suffolk	307,758	100.56	173.66
Mid Sussex	1,442,432	117.07	201.95
Middlesbrough	1,540,524	98.66	170.37
Milton Keynes	1,229,471	114.35	198.30
Mole Valley	278,432	113.82	196.54
New Forest	726,720	126.10	217.76
Newark and Sherwood	555,099	87.56	151.19
Newcastle under Lyme	755,700	78.70	150.86
Newcastle upon Tyne	3,540,011	85.76	148.09
Newham	3,270,945	223.51	346.99
North Cornwall	785,134	95.06	164.14
North Devon	761,263	109.95	189.66
North Dorset	442,945	100.71	173.73
North East Derby	555,051	79.87	141.45
North East Lincoln	1,425,452	85.81	153.36
North Hertfordshire	804,148	115.06	204.65
North Kesteven	477,640	87.53	151.13
North Lincolnshire	1,017,814	83.07	143.97
North Norfolk	694,904	92.45	159.84
North Shropshire	279,310	86.90	151.02
North Somerset	1,113,123	115.92	200.17
North Tyneside	1,964,942	80.25	139.34
North Warwickshire	437,768	91.58	160.70
North West Leicestershire	372,649	86.63	149.59
North Wiltshire	623,597	100.71	173.73
Northampton	2,002,351	113.90	196.67
Norwich	1,147,991	90.26	156.40
Nottingham	2,783,167	83.96	144.99
Nuneaton and Bedworth	822,002	88.81	154.92
Oadby and Wigston	286,631	85.39	148.27
Oldham	1,908,799	83.75	153.13
Oswestry	187,813	89.56	154.65
Oxford	866,910	122.71	213.93
Pendle	753,190	87.23	150.64
Penwith	812,198	94.58	173.40
Peterborough	1,499,900	114.08	197.00
Plymouth	2,452,020	92.07	158.97
Poole	1,072,501	104.52	191.62
Portsmouth	1,561,051	111.09	191.81
Preston	984,115	94.99	164.01
Purbeck	216,233	116.19	200.62
Reading	1,238,833	135.67	234.27
Redbridge	1,493,193	223.51	352.76
Redcar and Cleveland	1,486,136	94.34	162.90
Redditch	571,209	100.51	173.57
Reigate and Banstead	513,075	131.92	227.79
Restormel	927,144	108.16	186.57
Ribble Valley	160,730	81.96	141.52
Richmond upon Thames	971,006	223.51	346.99
Richmondshire	179,836	97.21	167.85
Rochdale	3,608,972	87.10	150.41
Rochford	353,263	103.82	179.26
Rossendale	570,634	88.21	152.16
Rother	655,384	117.07	201.95
Rotherham	1,793,414	73.64	132.52

(SI 2007 No.26, Sch 1)

	Administration subsidy Threshold (£)	Non-HRA Rent Rebates Cap (£)	(£)
Rugby	542,118	94.15	163.62
Runnymede	312,692	138.57	239.29
Rushcliffe	364,891	96.48	168.17
Rushmoor	421,480	117.07	201.95
Rutland	101,833	102.90	177.70
Ryedale	364,478	83.08	152.54
Salford	2,769,586	96.36	166.39
Salisbury	481,187	121.97	216.09
Sandwell	2,939,378	103.71	180.64
Scarborough	1,061,827	98.94	170.84
Sedgefield	892,905	85.26	147.64
Sedgemoor	578,007	106.66	184.18
Sefton	2,523,338	98.01	169.49
Selby	550,697	92.79	160.24
Sevenoaks	684,206	117.07	201.95
Sheffield	4,342,187	83.75	144.74
Shepway	753,323	107.33	185.33
Shrewsbury and Atcham	655,452	95.11	164.24
Slough	869,970	122.26	213.37
Solihull	963,097	99.57	171.94
South Bedfordshire	489,805	119.67	207.86
South Bucks	715,344	117.07	201.95
South Cambridgeshire	408,947	119.89	207.03
South Derbyshire	353,337	94.21	162.67
South Gloucestershire	2,774,785	102.68	180.81
South Hams	786,066	100.71	173.73
South Holland	575,231	89.35	154.30
South Kesteven	514,260	92.28	161.34
South Lakeland	453,490	106.13	188.71
South Norfolk	573,411	97.21	167.85
South Northamptonshire	201,640	106.08	184.62
South Oxfordshire	535,396	117.07	201.95
South Ribble	655,774	94.42	162.87
South Shropshire	236,887	92.82	160.12
South Somerset	820,781	100.71	173.73
South Staffordshire	744,790	92.82	160.12
South Tyneside	1,868,061	78.12	136.67
Southampton	1,772,938	98.03	188.07
Southend on Sea	1,451,034	106.44	183.80
Southwark	5,314,651	223.51	346.99
Spelthorne	446,961	117.07	201.95
St Albans	537,738	118.06	205.35
St Edmundsbury	524,174	106.04	183.78
St Helens	1,706,323	100.64	173.78
Stafford	681,083	92.82	160.12
Staffordshire Moorlands	459,312	90.27	155.71
Stevenage	566,404	116.92	201.89
Stockport	1,508,996	85.47	164.34
Stockton on Tees	1,303,882	89.51	155.97
Stoke on Trent	2,999,929	89.33	154.24
Stratford on Avon	575,445	92.82	160.12
Stroud	617,771	107.03	184.81
Suffolk Coastal	593,364	97.13	168.14
Sunderland	4,104,354	97.04	167.40
Surrey Heath	246,977	117.07	201.95
Sutton	937,379	223.51	346.99
Swale	988,384	117.07	201.95
Swindon	891,670	95.38	166.55
Tameside	1,983,153	99.17	171.06
Tamworth	391,561	97.36	169.29
Tandridge	250,169	116.83	203.44

Income-related Benefits (Subsidy to Authorities) (Misc Amends and Electronic Comms) Order 2007

	Administration subsidy Threshold (£)	Non-HRA Rent Rebates Cap (£)	(£)
Taunton Deane	785,620	94.94	163.94
Teesdale	141,953	87.05	150.31
Teignbridge	904,466	112.26	193.86
Telford and Wrekin	1,252,063	92.82	160.12
Tendring	1,052,313	98.00	179.86
Test Valley	472,663	113.80	196.29
Tewkesbury	351,544	92.87	160.20
Thanet	1,560,632	106.35	183.64
Three Rivers	348,065	120.56	209.77
Thurrock	910,565	113.49	195.95
Tonbridge and Malling	605,472	117.07	201.95
Torbay	1,319,475	103.66	178.81
Torridge	463,075	102.57	177.11
Tower Hamlets	4,313,752	223.51	374.38
Trafford	1,304,835	95.94	165.66
Tunbridge Wells	655,838	117.07	201.95
Tynedale	356,005	93.57	161.41
Uttlesford	283,576	117.32	202.66
Vale of White Horse	446,705	117.07	201.95
Vale Royal	1,056,871	94.94	163.95
Wakefield	2,009,095	83.83	156.34
Walsall	2,722,971	95.48	164.89
Waltham Forest	2,188,169	223.51	367.87
Wandsworth	2,402,306	223.51	390.57
Wansbeck	490,155	74.07	127.90
Warrington	1,265,550	95.33	164.61
Warwick	659,071	101.13	176.96
Watford	480,458	117.41	202.72
Waveney	1,015,793	92.30	159.38
Waverley	429,795	127.22	219.45
Wealden	557,215	99.81	191.49
Wear Valley	629,981	86.22	148.87
Wellingborough	361,833	93.99	162.29
Welwyn Hatfield	535,731	110.25	193.38
West Berkshire	905,001	117.07	201.95
West Devon	265,001	100.71	173.73
West Dorset	546,291	100.71	173.73
West Lancashire	934,290	89.13	155.22
West Lindsey	491,595	86.71	149.91
West Oxfordshire	420,810	112.22	193.59
West Somerset	283,361	100.71	173.73
West Wiltshire	658,210	115.04	198.44
Westminster	2,260,565	223.51	428.82
Weymouth and Portland	613,230	104.29	179.90
Wigan	2,162,909	89.41	154.39
Winchester	399,158	117.53	202.95
Windsor and Maidenhead	768,568	117.07	201.95
Wirral	2,975,390	104.37	180.21
Woking	346,099	151.4	261.45
Wokingham	305,817	118.29	210.01
Wolverhampton	2,283,266	86.71	160.13
Worcester	592,374	89.41	156.05
Worthing	610,368	117.07	201.95
Wychavon	654,519	116.85	201.54
Wycombe	630,922	134.52	232.29
Wyre	785,444	94.80	163.52
Wyre Forest	798,083	96.56	166.56
York	802,154	98.23	169.61

	Administration subsidy Threshold (£)	Non-HRA Rent Rebates Cap (£)	(£)
Wales			
Blaenau Gwent	799,019	91.65	158.24
Bridgend	988,768	93.01	160.62
Caerphilly	1,250,336	98.31	169.76
Cardiff	2,228,733	103.42	179.59
Carmarthenshire	1,180,478	89.75	154.98
Ceredigion	379,744	98.37	169.86
Conwy	1,792,884	86.52	156.20
Denbighshire	630,626	84.15	146.72
Flintshire	797,706	89.49	154.73
Gwynedd	753,834	89.13	153.90
Isle of Anglesey	669,910	87.88	151.74
Merthyr Tydfil	817,642	89.17	153.98
Monmouthshire	475,585	103.25	179.51
Neath Port Talbot	1,124,438	90.39	156.09
Newport	1,012,024	97.89	171.18
Pembrokeshire	851,138	87.86	151.70
Powys	725,790	92.14	159.35
Rhondda Cynon Taff	1,987,547	87.70	151.44
Swansea	1,737,342	93.70	161.81
Torfaen	627,677	101.74	177.30
Vale of Glamorgan	807,675	105.59	182.34
Wrexham	891,479	83.92	145.37
Scotland			
Aberdeen	1,488,421	79.65	139.02
Aberdeenshire	1,162,226	75.09	133.40
Angus	932,799	70.27	126.75
Argyll and Bute	606,884	85.63	147.88
Clackmannanshire	419,879	75.46	139.24
Comhairle nan Eilean Siar	183,493	88.56	154.86
Dumfries and Galloway	1,315,712	80.33	141.23
Dundee	2,072,708	87.31	152.30
East Ayrshire	1,136,017	76.85	132.82
East Dunbartonshire	453,465	82.14	145.45
East Lothian	5,435,595	73.87	127.56
East Renfrewshire	354,131	78.82	144.59
Edinburgh	4,324,973	100.39	173.35
Falkirk	1,101,183	80.03	147.09
Fife	2,807,442	76.13	136.38
Glasgow	11,743,523	101.72	175.65
Highland	1,369,487	93.42	161.30
Inverclyde	922,614	95.55	170.47
Midlothian	762,226	66.98	115.67
Moray	449,823	67.74	116.96
North Ayrshire	1,390,101	71.99	127.46
North Lanarkshire	3,005,055	83.85	146.60
Orkney Islands	94,955	78.51	135.56
Perth & Kinross	734,348	71.28	123.09
Renfrewshire	1,918,068	87.13	158.90
Scottish Borders	828,671	75.83	130.93
Shetland	84,568	102.20	176.47
South Ayrshire	908,735	78.20	135.01
South Lanarkshire	2,633,563	85.82	148.19
Stirling	544,644	80.89	139.66
West Dunbartonshire	1,212,914	80.57	139.14
West Lothian	1,547,073	82.78	169.42"

SCHEDULE 2
Articles 4(4)
SCHEDULE TO BE INSERTED AS SCHEDULE 6 TO THE PRINCIPAL ORDER

" SCHEDULE 6
Articles 3A
ELECTRONIC COMMUNICATIONS
PART 1

INTERPRETATION

Interpretation
1. In this Schedule "official computer system" means a computer system maintained by or on behalf of the Secretary of State for the sending, receipt, processing or storage of any claim or return.

PART 2

ELECTRONIC COMMUNICATIONS – GENERAL PROVISIONS

Conditions for the use of electronic communications
2.–(1) An authority or auditor must use an approved method of–
(a) electronic communication;
(b) authenticating the identity of the sender of the communication;
(c) authenticating any claim or return delivered by means of an electronic communication; and
(d) submitting to the Secretary of State any claim or return.
(2) An authority or auditor must submit any claim or return by means of an electronic communication in an approved form.
(3) Where a claim or return is submitted electronically but not in accordance with the conditions specified in this paragraph, that claim or return shall be treated as not having been submitted.
(4) In this paragraph "approved" means approved by means of a direction given by the Secretary of State.

Use of intermediaries
3. The Secretary of State may–
(a) use intermediaries in connection with the receipt, authentication or security of any claim or return delivered by means of an electronic communication; and
(b) require authorities or auditors to use intermediaries in connection with those matters.

PART 3

ELECTRONIC COMMUNICATION – EVIDENTIAL PROVISIONS

Effect of delivering information by means of electronic communication
4.–(1) Any claim or return which is delivered by means of an electronic communication shall be treated as having been delivered in the approved manner or form on the day the conditions imposed–
(a) by or under this Schedule; and
(b) by or under Part II of this Order
are satisfied.
(2) The Secretary of State may, by a direction, determine that any claim or return is to be treated as delivered on a different day (whether earlier or later) from the day provided for in sub-paragraph (1).
(3) A claim or return shall not be treated as delivered to an official computer system by means of an electronic communication unless it is accepted by the system to which it is delivered.

Proof of identify of sender or recipient of information
5. For the purpose of any legal proceedings, it shall be presumed that the identity of the sender or recipient, as the case may be, of any claim or return delivered by means of an electronic communication to an official computer system is the same as is recorded on that official computer system.

Proof of delivery of information
6.–(1) For the purpose of any legal proceedings, it shall be presumed that–

(a) if the delivery of any claim or return has been recorded on an official computer system, the use of an electronic communication has resulted in the delivery of that claim or return to the Secretary of State;
(b) if the delivery of any claim or return submitted by means of an electronic communication to the Secretary of State has not been recorded on an official computer system, no delivery has been made;
(c) any claim or return submitted by means of an electronic communication has been received on the time and date recorded on an official computer system.

Proof of content of information
7. For the purpose of any legal proceedings, the content of any claim or return submitted by means of an electronic communication shall be presumed to be that recorded on an official computer system."

The Housing Benefit (Daily Liability Entitlement) Amendment Regulations 2007
(SI 2007 No. 294)

Citation and commencement
1. These Regulations may be cited as the Housing Benefit (Daily Liability Entitlement) Amendment Regulations 2007 and shall come into force on 1st April 2007.

Amendment of the Housing Benefit Regulations 2006
2.–(1) The Housing Benefit Regulations 2006 shall be amended as follows.
(2) In regulation 76 (date on which entitlement is to commence)–
(a) for paragraph (3)(c) substitute–

" (c) he becomes liable in that benefit week to make payments, which fall due on a daily basis, in respect of the accommodation listed in paragraph (4) which he occupies as his home."; and

(b) after regulation 76(3) insert–

" (4) The accommodation referred to in paragraph (3)(c) is–
(a) a hostel;
(b) board and lodging accommodation where the payments are to an authority under section 206(2) of the Housing Act 1996 or section 35(2)(b) of the Housing (Scotland) Act 1987;
(c) accommodation which the authority holds on a licence agreement where the payments are to an authority under section 206(2) of the Housing Act 1996 or section 35(2)(b) of the Housing (Scotland) Act 1987; or
(d) accommodation outside that authority's Housing Revenue Account which the authority holds on a lease granted for a term not exceeding 10 years.
(5) In this regulation–
"board and lodging accommodation" means–
(a) accommodation provided to a person or, if he is a member of a family, to him or any other member of his family, for a charge which is inclusive of the provision of that accommodation and at least some cooked or prepared meals which both are cooked or prepared (by a person other than a person to whom the accommodation is provided or by a member of his family) and are consumed in that accommodation or associated premises; or
(b) accommodation provided to a person in a hotel, guest house, lodging house or some similar establishment,

but it does not include accommodation in a care home, an Abbeyfield Home, an independent hospital or a hostel; and

"Housing Revenue Account" has the same meaning as for the purposes of Part VIII of the Social Security Administration Act 1992.".

(3) In regulation 79(8) (date on which change of circumstances is to take effect) omit the words "in respect of a hostel".

Amendment of the Housing Benefit (Persons who have attained the qualifying age for state pension credit) Regulations 2006
3.–(1) The Housing Benefit (Persons who have attained the qualifying age for state pension credit) Regulations 2006 shall be amended as follows.
(2) In regulation 57 (date on which entitlement is to commence)
(a) for paragraph (2)(b) substitute–

" (b) he becomes liable in that benefit week to make payments, which fall due on a daily basis, in respect of the accommodation listed in paragraph (3) which he occupies as his home."; and

(b) after regulation 57(2) insert–

" (3) The accommodation referred to in paragraph (2)(b) is–
(a) a hostel;
(b) board and lodging accommodation where the payments are to an authority under section 206(2) of the Housing Act 1996 or section 35(2)(b) of the Housing (Scotland) Act 1987;
(c) accommodation which the authority holds on a licence agreement where the payments are to an authority under section 206(2) of the Housing Act 1996 or section 35(2)(b) of the Housing (Scotland) Act 1987; or
(d) accommodation outside that authority's Housing Revenue Account which the authority holds on a lease granted for a term not exceeding 10 years.

(4) In this regulation–
"board and lodging accommodation" means–
(a) accommodation provided to a person or, if he is a member of a family, to him or any other member of his family, for a charge which is inclusive of the provision of that accommodation and at least some cooked or prepared meals which both are cooked or prepared (by a person other than a person to whom the accommodation is provided or by a member of his family) and are consumed in that accommodation or associated premises; or
(b) accommodation provided to a person in a hotel, guest house, lodging house or some similar establishment,

but it does not include accommodation in a care home, an Abbeyfield Home, an independent hospital or a hostel; and

"Housing Revenue Account" has the same meaning as for the purposes of Part VIII of the Social Security Administration Act 1992.".

(3) In regulation 59(8) (date on which change of circumstances is to take effect) omit the words "in respect of a hostel".

The Rent Repayment Orders (Supplementary Provisions) (England) Regulations 2007
(SI 2007 No. 572)

Citation, commencement, application and interpretation
1.–(1) These Regulations may be cited as the Rent Repayment Orders (Supplementary Provisions) (England) Regulations 2007 and shall come into force on 6th April 2007.
(2) These Regulations apply in relation to England only.
(3) In these Regulations, "the Act" means the Housing Act 2004.

Overpayments of housing benefit
2.–(1) Paragraph (2) applies if, in the course of proceedings on an application under subsection (5) of section 73 of the Act (other consequences of operating unlicensed HMOs: rent repayment orders) or subsection (5) of section 96 of the Act (other consequences of operating unlicensed houses: rent repayment orders), it comes to the notice of the local housing authority that in respect of periodical payments payable in connection with occupation of the part or parts of the HMO or of the whole or part of the house to which the application applies there may have been a payment of housing benefit that was not properly payable.
(2) A local housing authority may apply to the residential property tribunal for leave to amend their application by substituting for the total amount of housing benefit paid, such part of that amount as they believe is properly payable.
(3) For the purposes of paragraphs (1) and (2)–
(a) an amount of housing benefit is properly payable if the person to whom, or in respect of whom, it is paid is entitled to it under the Housing Benefit Regulations 2006 or the Housing Benefit (Persons who have attained the qualifying age for state pension credit) Regulations 2006 (whether on the initial decision or as subsequently revised or superseded or further revised or superseded), and
(b) "overpayment of housing benefit" has the meaning given by regulation 99 of the Housing Benefit Regulations 2006 or, as the case may be, regulation 80 of the Housing Benefit (Persons who have obtained the qualifying age for state pension credit) Regulations 2006.

3.–(1) Subject to paragraph (3), a local housing authority may apply an amount recovered under a rent repayment order for any of the purposes mentioned in paragraph (2).
(2) The purposes are the reimbursement of the authority's costs and expenses (whether administrative or legal) incurred in, or associated with–
(a) the making of the application under section 73(5) of the Act or, as the case may be, section 96(5) of the Act;
(b) the registration and enforcement of any legal charge under section 74(9)(b) or 97(9)(b) of the Act on the relevant property;
(c) dealing with any application for the grant of a licence in respect of the relevant property under Part 2 of the Act (licensing of HMOs) or, as the case may be, Part 3 of the Act (selective licensing of other residential accommodation);
(d) the prosecution of the appropriate person for an offence under section 72(1) of the Act or, as the case may be, section 95(1) of the Act, in relation to the relevant property (whether proceedings are instituted before or after the making of the order);
(e) the making of an interim or final management order under Chapter 1 of Part 4 of the Act (interim and final management orders) in respect of the relevant

property (whether the management order is made before or after the making of the rent repayment order);
(f) the management of the relevant property while an interim or final management order is in force;
(g) the execution of works undertaken in relation to the relevant property while an interim management order is in force; and
(h) the preparation of, or execution of works under, a management scheme under section 119 of the Act (management schemes and accounts) while a final management order is in force.

(3) Nothing in paragraph (1) authorises the application of an amount by way of reimbursement of an authority's costs or expenses where a court or residential property tribunal has made an order with respect to all or some of those costs or expenses.

(4) In paragraph (2), "the relevant property" means the HMO or house to which the rent repayment order relates.

Treatment of surpluses
4. An amount recovered under a rent repayment order which is not applied for a purpose mentioned in regulation 3(2), shall be paid into the Consolidated Fund.

The Social Security (Miscellaneous Amendments) Regulations 2007
(SI 2007 No. 719)

Citation, commencement and interpretation
1.–(1) These Regulations may be cited as the Social Security (Miscellaneous Amendments) Regulations 2007.

(2) This regulation and regulations 2(1), (3) to (6), (7)(b)(ii) and (e), (8)(a), (9) and 3(1), (3) to (7), (8)(d) and (j), (9)(a), (11) and 4, 6 to 9 shall come into force on 2nd April 2007.

Amendment of the Housing Benefit Regulations 2006
6.–(1) The Housing Benefit Regulations 2006 are amended as follows.

(2) For regulation 42(2)(d) (notional income) substitute–

" (d) any sum to which paragraph 45(2)(a) of Schedule 6 (capital to be disregarded) applies which is administered in the way referred to in paragraph 45(1)(a);
(da) any sum to which paragraph 46(a) of Schedule 6 refers;".

(3) For regulation 49(2)(e) (notional capital) substitute–

" (e) any sum to which paragraph 45(2)(a) of Schedule 6 (capital to be disregarded) applies which is administered in the way referred to in paragraph 45(1)(a); or
(ea) any sum to which paragraph 46(a) of Schedule 6 refers; or".

(4) For regulation 87 (amendment and withdrawal of claim) substitute–

" **Amendment and withdrawal of claim**
87.–(1) A person who has made a claim may amend it at any time before a decision has been made on it, by a notice in writing delivered or sent to the designated office, except where the claim was made by telephone in accordance with regulation 83(4A) where the amendment may be made by telephone, and any claim so amended shall be treated as if it had been amended in the first instance.

(2) A person who has made a claim may withdraw it at any time before a decision has been made on it, by notice to the designated office, and any such notice of withdrawal shall have effect when it is received.".

(5) In Schedule 1 (ineligible service charges) for paragraph 1(a)(iii) substitute–

" (iii) leisure items such as either sports facilities (except a children's play area), or television rental, licence and subscription fees (except radio relay charges and charges made in respect of the conveyance and installation and maintenance of equipment for the conveyance of a television broadcasting service);".

(6) In paragraph 14(6) of Schedule 3 (severe disability premium), for "the date on which the award is made" substitute "the date on which the award is first paid".

Amendment of the Housing Benefit (Persons who have attained the qualifying age for state pension credit) Regulations 2006
7.–(1) The Housing Benefit (Persons who have attained the qualifying age for state pension credit) Regulations 2006 are amended as follows.

(2) For regulation 68 (amendment and withdrawal of claim) substitute–

" **Amendment and withdrawal of claim**
68.–(1) A person who has made a claim may amend it at any time before a decision has been made on it, by a notice in writing delivered or sent to the designated office, except where the claim was made by telephone in accordance with regulation

64(5A) where the amendment may be made by telephone, and any claim so amended shall be treated as if it had been amended in the first instance.

(2)   A person who has made a claim may withdraw it at any time before a decision has been made on it, by notice to the designated office, and any such notice of withdrawal shall have effect when it is received.".

(3)   In Schedule 1 (ineligible service charges) for paragraph 1(a)(iii) substitute–

" (iii)   leisure items such as either sports facilities (except a children's play area), or television rental, licence and subscription fees (except radio relay charges and charges made in respect of the conveyance and installation and maintenance of equipment for the conveyance of a television broadcasting service);".

(4)   In paragraph 6(8)(a) of Schedule 3 (severe disability premium), for "the date on which the award is made" substitute "the date on which the award is first paid".

Amendment of the Council Tax Benefit Regulations 2006

8.–(1)   The Council Tax Benefit Regulations 2006 are amended as follows.

(2)   For regulation 32(2)(d) (notional income) substitute–

" (d)   any sum to which paragraph 47(2)(a) of Schedule 5 (capital to be disregarded) applies which is administered in the way referred to in paragraph 47(1)(a);
(da)   any sum to which paragraph 48(a) of Schedule 5 refers;".

(3)   For regulation 39(2)(e) (notional capital) substitute–

" (e)   any sum to which paragraph 47(2)(a) of Schedule 5 (capital to be disregarded) applies which is administered in the way referred to in paragraph 47(1)(a); or
(ea)   any sum to which paragraph 48(a) of Schedule 5 refers; or".

(4)   For regulation 73 (amendment and withdrawal of claim) substitute–

" **Amendment and withdrawal of claim**

73.–(1)   A person who has made a claim may amend it at any time before a decision has been made on it, by a notice in writing delivered or sent to the designated office, except where the claim was made by telephone in accordance with regulation 69(4A) where the amendment may be made by telephone, and any claim so amended shall be treated as if it had been amended in the first instance.

(2)   A person who has made a claim may withdraw it at any time before a decision has been made on it, by notice to the designated office, and any such notice of withdrawal shall have effect when it is received.".

(5)   In paragraph 14(6) of Schedule 1 for (severe disability premium), "the date on which the award is made" substitute "the date on which the award is first paid".

Amendment of the Council Tax Benefit (Persons who have attained the qualifying age for state pension credit) Regulations 2006

9.–(1)   The Council Tax Benefit (Persons who have attained the qualifying age for state pension credit) Regulations 2006 are amended as follows.

(2)   For regulation 58 (amendment and withdrawal of claim) substitute–

" **Amendment and withdrawal of claim**

58.–(1)   A person who has made a claim may amend it at any time before a decision has been made on it, by a notice in writing delivered or sent to the designated office, except where the claim was made by telephone in accordance with regulation 53(4A) where the amendment may be made by telephone, and any claim so amended shall be treated as if it had been amended in the first instance.

(2) A person who has made a claim may withdraw it at any time before a decision has been made on it, by notice to the designated office, and any such notice of withdrawal shall have effect when it is received.".

(3) In paragraph 6(8)(a) of Schedule 1 (severe disability premium), for "the date on which the award is made" substitute "the date on which the award is first paid".

The Income-related Benefits (Subsidy to Authorities) Amendment Order 2007
(SI 2007 No. 731)

Citation, commencement, interpretation and extent
1.–(1) This Order may be cited as the Income-related Benefits (Subsidy to Authorities) Amendment Order 2007 and shall come into force on 1st April 2007.

(2) In this Order, "the 1998 Order" means the Income-related Benefits (Subsidy to Authorities) Order 1998.

(3) This Order extends to England and Wales.

Amendment of the 1998 Order
2. Schedule 4A to the 1998 Order (rent rebate limitation deductions) is amended in accordance with the Schedule to this Order.

SCHEDULE 1
Article 2

AMENDMENTS TO SCHEDULE 4A TO THE 1998 ORDER
1. In paragraph 2 (England – liability to deduction), for sub-paragraphs (6) and (7) there shall be substituted–

" (6) (6) The RPI figure for the period beginning with September 2001 and ending with September of the year prior to the relevant year is 1.1663.

(7) The annual factor for 2007-08 is 0.4.".

2. In paragraph 3(amount of deduction), for sub-paragraph (3) there shall be substituted–

" (3) The rebate proportion for each year commencing with 2007-08 is 0.77.".

3. For Part 3 there shall be substituted–

" PART 3
WEEKLY RENT LIMITS FOR PURPOSES OF PART 2: AUTHORITIES IN ENGLAND

RELEVANT YEAR 2007-08

Authority	Weekly rent limit	Authority	Weekly rent limit
Adur	66.34	Bolsover	53.11
Alnwick	51.35	Bolton	51.89
Arun	70.81	Bournemouth	61.45
Ashfield	48.78	Bracknell Forest	70.86
Ashford	67.47	Braintree	65.52
Aylesbury Vale	71.81	Brent	82.88
Babergh	63.94	Brentwood	70.10
Barking and Dagenham	65.19	Bridgnorth	62.20
Barnet	77.23	Brighton and Hove	61.62
Barnsley	51.11	Bristol	57.59
Barrow in Furness	57.17	Broxtowe	62.82
Basildon	62.19	Bury	56.57
Bassetlaw	53.06	Cambridge	69.60
Berwick upon Tweed	49.72	Camden	86.42
Birmingham	59.44	Cannock Chase	56.54
Blaby	53.99	Canterbury	66.10
Blackpool	51.07	Caradon	54.03
Blyth Valley	47.11	Carrick	52.16

The Income-related Benefits (Subsidy to Authorities) Amendment Order 2007

Authority	Weekly rent limit	Authority	Weekly rent limit
Castle Morpeth	51.74	Kensington and Chelsea	92.15
Castle Point	68.93	Kettering	57.24
Charnwood	52.62	Kings Lynn and West Norfolk	56.71
Cheltenham	61.66	Kingston upon Hull	53.10
Chesterfield	54.17	Kingston upon Thames	84.77
Chester-le-Street	51.30	Kirklees	53.16
Chorley	51.49	Lambeth	76.96
City of London	79.30	Lancaster	55.86
City of York	58.47	Leeds	52.30
Colchester	63.33	Leicester	54.17
Corby	54.45	Lewes	65.54
Crawley	71.30	Lewisham	69.36
Croydon	81.52	Lincoln	48.63
Dacorum	71.95	Liverpool	56.95
Darlington	52.24	Luton	61.34
Dartford	65.86	Macclesfield	60.27
Daventry	61.09	Manchester	59.56
Derby	55.69	Mansfield	52.76
Derwentside	53.53	Medway Towns	60.29
Doncaster	51.02	Melton	53.97
Dover	65.26	Merton	76.86
Dudley	59.17	Mid Devon	60.23
Durham	52.36	Mid Suffolk	60.57
Ealing	80.92	Milton Keynes	60.05
Easington	50.28	Mole Valley	74.00
East Devon	57.42	New Forest	71.94
East Riding	54.95	Newark and Sherwood	55.05
Eastbourne	57.87	Newcastle upon Tyne	53.10
Ellesmere Port and Neston	53.76	Newham	68.72
Enfield	74.47	Northampton	59.01
Epping Forest	70.61	North Cornwall	55.35
Exeter	54.40	North East Derbyshire	53.83
Fareham	65.66	North Kesteven	55.36
Fenland	60.63	North Lincolnshire	52.59
Gateshead	53.74	North Norfolk	57.79
Gedling	52.64	North Shropshire	56.49
Gloucester	59.53	North Somerset	55.35
Gosport	63.20	North Tyneside	51.97
Gravesham	66.11	North Warwickshire	59.29
Great Yarmouth	52.75	North West Leicestershire	55.09
Greenwich	72.98	Norwich	56.32
Guildford	78.31	Nottingham	52.99
Hackney	76.25	Nuneaton and Bedworth	55.08
Hammersmith and Fulham	81.45	Oadby and Wigston	54.99
Harborough	59.59	Oldham	52.00
Haringey	78.53	Oswestry	56.34
Harlow	65.55	Oxford	72.25
Harrogate	61.25	Pendle	51.98
Harrow	85.50	Plymouth	49.18
Havering	67.02	Poole	62.61
High Peak	54.56	Portsmouth	61.30
Hillingdon	85.18	Reading	78.84
Hinckley and Bosworth	54.98	Redbridge	81.65
Hounslow	75.89	Redditch	56.76
Hyndburn	53.39	Ribble Valley	52.40
Ipswich	58.20	Richmondshire	57.34
Isles of Scilly	61.04	Rochdale	53.10
Islington	83.34	Rochford	64.37

(SI 2007 No.731, Sch 1)

Authority	Weekly rent limit	Authority	Weekly rent limit
Rossendale	52.44	Sutton	73.84
Rotherham	50.42	Swindon	58.21
Rugby	57.37	Tamworth	58.67
Runnymede	79.37	Tandridge	69.79
Rutland	59.33	Taunton Deane	58.89
Salford	56.99	Teesdale	53.05
Salisbury	68.31	Tendring	60.16
Sandwell	61.31	Thanet	61.82
Sedgefield	50.92	Three Rivers	73.64
Sedgemoor	59.51	Thurrock	62.03
Sefton	58.64	Torridge	53.10
Selby	57.27	Tower Hamlets	75.91
Sheffield	50.50	Uttlesford	71.92
Shepway	62.57	Waltham Forest	71.25
Slough	76.74	Wandsworth	88.74
Solihull	60.15	Wansbeck	46.96
South Bedfordshire	70.02	Warrington	55.08
South Cambridgeshire	70.87	Warwick	65.14
South Derbyshire	56.62	Watford	72.72
South Gloucestershire	63.23	Waveney	56.91
South Holland	53.44	Waverley	77.60
South Kesteven	54.81	Wealden	61.49
South Lakeland	61.94	Wear Valley	52.16
South Northants	67.67	Wellingborough	56.04
South Tyneside	51.09	Welwyn Hatfield	71.78
Southampton	60.64	West Lancashire	54.13
Southend-on-Sea	63.69	Westminster	91.55
Southwark	75.27	Wigan	53.79
St Albans	76.45	Winchester	74.09
Stevenage	71.50	Woking	77.96
Stockport	52.45	Wokingham	76.94
Stockton on Tees	55.76	Wolverhampton	54.93
Stoke-on-Trent	53.27	Wycombe	77.77''
Stroud	61.56		

The Income-related Benefits (Subsidy to Authorities) Amendment Order 2007

For Part 5 there shall be substituted–

"*PART 5*

AMOUNTS FOR PURPOSES OF PART 4, PARAGRAPH 4: AUTHORITIES IN WALES
RELEVANT YEAR 2007-08

Authority	(1) Specified amount "O"	(2) Guideline rent increase
Blaenau Gwent	48.43	1.74
Caerphilly	54.16	2.62
Cardiff	60.25	3.20
Carmarthenshire	50.60	3.03
Ceredigion	54.08	2.48
Conwy	53.01	3.52
Denbighshire	49.26	2.73
Flintshire	51.55	3.13
Gwynedd	51.27	3.07
Isle of Anglesey	49.74	2.48
Merthyr Tydfil	46.99	3.22
Monmouthshire	58.36	2.67
Neath Port Talbot	49.62	2.21
Newport	55.55	2.91
Pembrokeshire	50.72	3.12
Powys	53.96	2.51
Rhondda, Cynon, Taff	49.87	2.29
Swansea	52.07	2.67
Torfaen	56.45	2.79
Vale of Glamorgan	57.99	2.67
Wrexham	49.42	3.26"